There are many stories of war and military leadership that make us admire our men and women in uniform. However, this book explores the unique story of how five friends, including two sets of brothers, all became generals. The probability of this happening is almost zero, and yet it happened. What the book reveals is that ultimately leadership is a team sport. These five generals prove that if you build the right team early in your career, everyone on the team can achieve greatness.

—**WILLIAM A. FREY**, PRINCIPAL AND CEO
OF GREENWICH FINANCIAL SERVICES AND
AUTHOR OF *WAY TOO BIG TO FAIL: HOW
GOVERNMENT AND PRIVATE INDUSTRY CAN
BUILD A FAIL-SAFE MORTGAGE SYSTEM*

LEADERSHIP FROM 30,000 FEET

ATTRIBUTES OF EFFECTIVE LEADERS AS TOLD BY FIVE AIR FORCE GENERALS

H. D. "JAKE" POLUMBO   ROB POLUMBO

TOM JONES   JAMES J. JONES

RICHARD "BEEF" HADDAD

Edited and compiled by Blake Atwood with BA Writing Solutions LLC: blakeatwood.com.

ISBN: 9781090451422

INTRODUCTION

Through the pages of this book, you'll come to know five men—Jake, Mumbles, Rev, Honez, and Beef—who ascended the ranks of the US Air Force to become generals. Combined, they have more than one hundred years of high-level leadership experience that encompasses the globe and have been responsible for leading tens of thousands of active duty and reservist US Air Force service members.

In other words, they know how to lead because they've been leading others for decades. But each general would also be the first to tell you, "No leader leads well without great teams, and I am the leader I am today because of the leaders who have led me."

Consequently, this book contains both personal anecdotes and stories about the men and women who've led these generals and who've served alongside these generals. These profiles in leadership have been gleaned through their decades of service and leadership.

When the five generals were asked to provide what they think it means to be an effective leader, they discovered striking similarities within their very different stories. One general was forced to eject from an F-16. Another hailed the harrowing landing of a damaged U-2. Yet another anxiously awaited the imminent impact of a nearby missile on the first night of Operation Iraqi Freedom. Through these events and more, the men saw how the major attributes of an effective leader fell into five distinct categories: commitment, courage, competence, compassion, and character.

Consequently, this book is divided into five sections, and each general provides an essay for each attribute. This gives you at least five compelling stories per leadership characteristic. The stories are presented as each general can best recall them, though careful liberties have been taken with regard to remembered conversations.

Additionally, while three leadership takeaways are presented at the end of each chapter, a majority of the chapters are story-driven, with little direct guidance as to how to lead. In other words, this isn't a guidebook for leadership; it's encouragement to become an effective leader by way of emulating great leaders.

Although the five generals have retired from active duty, they are all still passionate about helping others lead well. That's why they formed Two Blue Aces LLC, a leadership consulting company that advises businesses around the world. Together, they specialize in strategic reviews, business plan development, and leadership and mentor training.

Now, meet the generals:

Major General USAF (Ret) H. D. "Jake" Polumbo is a founding partner of Two Blue Aces LLC. After thirty-four years of service, he retired in 2015 as the commander of the Ninth Air Force in South Carolina, comprising eight active-duty wings in the southeastern US with more than four hundred aircraft and over 29,000 active-duty and civilian personnel. He is also Rob Polumbo's brother.

Major General USAF (Ret) Rob "Mumbles" Polumbo is a senior consultant with Two Blue Aces LLC. After thirty-two years of service, he retired as the special assistant to the commander, Air Force Reserve Command, Robins Air Force Base. He assisted and advised the commander on the daily operations of the command, consisting of approximately seventy thousand citizen airmen and more than three hundred aircraft among three numbered air forces. He is also Jake Polumbo's brother.

Lieutenant General USAF (Ret) Tom "Honez" Jones is a senior consultant with Two Blue Aces LLC. After thirty-five years of service, he retired as the vice commander of US Air Forces in Europe/Air Forces Africa, where he was second-in-command for the air component to U.S. European Command and U.S. Africa Command. He was responsible for providing full-spectrum warfighting capabilities throughout the entire area of responsibility, which encompassed 104 countries in Europe, Africa, and the Arctic and Atlantic Oceans. He executed the organization, training, and equipping of over 35,000 members at seven operating bases in five European nations. He is also Jim Jones's brother.

Major General USAF (Ret) Jim "Rev" Jones is a senior consultant with Two Blue Aces LLC. After thirty-one years of service, he retired as the assistant deputy chief of staff for Operations, Plans and Requirements, where he was responsible to the secretary of the Air Force and the chief of staff for formulating policy supporting air, space, irregular warfare, counter-proliferation, homeland security, weather and cyber operations. As the Air Force operations deputy to the joint chiefs of staff, General Jones helped determine operational requirements, capabilities, and training necessary to support national security objectives and military strategy. He is also Tom Jones's brother.

Major General USAF (Ret) Richard "Beef" Haddad is a senior consultant with Two Blue Aces LLC. After thirty-five years of service, he retired as vice commander, Air Force Reserve Command. While working in the Air Force Reserve, he served as deputy chief in the Pentagon and directed Planning and Programming. Additionally, General Haddad sat on the Air Force board that plans, programs, budgets, and executes future warfighting capabilities for the Air Force. He is also like a brother to the Polumbo brothers.

One set of brothers becoming USAF generals is uncommon. Two sets of brothers, all of whom know each other, becoming USAF generals is a rarity. The fact that these men led alongside each other for decades—and that they still like talking to each other—is extraordinary.

They were commanders in the states as well as overseas in combat zones. They have served at the Pentagon and on major commands in the Air Force. The four brothers flew F-16s for most of their careers. Four of the five generals attended the US Air Force Academy. Three of them graduated from the prestigious and challenging Weapons and Tactics School. In fact, Mumbles attended the school when Jake and Rev were instructors there.

To chart how these generals have come to know and rely upon each other over the decades they've known each other would require more pages than an introduction needs. Suffice it to say: you may encounter common themes and conclusions within these pages because these men have had similar experiences for years. However, considering that they've all successfully led upper-echelon teams across the globe, maybe the similarities aren't due to their background. Maybe there truly are foundational aspects to leadership they each witnessed time and again.

The five generals of Two Blue Aces LLC hope that the following stories both encourage and challenge you to become an effective leader.

PART 1

COMMITMENT

CHAPTER 1

NEAR ROCKS, FAR ROCKS

ROB "MUMBLES" POLUMBO

"To embark on the journey towards your goals and dreams requires bravery. To remain on that path requires courage. The bridge that merges the two is commitment." —Steve Maraboli

---

I STARTED my career as a fighter pilot flying a couple hundred feet above the ground at six hundred miles per hour, velocities approaching the speed of sound. Such flying was wrought with danger since any deviation or delayed reaction by only a few seconds could result in a deadly ground impact.

If your jet strikes the ground at those speeds, the grim reality is that your probability of dying rapidly approaches 100 percent.

Consequently, as new fighter pilots, one of the first concepts we were taught by our instructors was a simple tool to successfully aviate, navigate, and communicate while flying close to terrain at a thousand feet per second. The premise of "near rocks, far rocks" prioritized the numerous tasks an aviator had to accomplish to successfully get to and from a target at very low altitudes and very high speeds.

The highest priority was always to clear the rocks closest to your flight path. Only after you were assured of safe passage over the immediate "near rocks" could you then perform the secondary tasks of flying in formation, working the radar, avoiding threats, and finding the target. These tasks, along with planning to navigate around the upcoming "far rocks," were performed in a cadence, a.k.a. "crosscheck" in aviation terminology.

"Near rocks, far rocks" also cemented a contract between the flight leader and the wingmen to work in unison to successfully obtain their mission objectives. The members of the flight were committed to and trusted each other to perform their tasked responsibilities. This bond, which I learned at an early age as a fighter pilot, developed into a devotion to team commitment that would guide me for the rest of my life.

To provide perspective on the planning and execution of a high-threat, low-level flight, consider the following start-to-finish recap of a mission I routinely flew while training for a Cold War combat scenario.

As flight leader, I'd start my planning several days in advance by visiting the squadron intelligence office to determine a realistic scenario and to receive the latest threat assessments of Soviet air defense systems. The intel experts had developed the scenario to include a simulated target and an array of air-to-air and surface-to-air threats I could expect en route. Using this information, I'd prepare a tactical plan to minimize our risk of detection and engagement with enemy forces while maximizing our chances of destroying the intended target.

Our overall objectives were simple: "Kill and survive!"

Still, extensive planning had to be done. The process included choosing a route to and from the target area (the ingress and egress routes, respectively) that used the terrain's features to degrade the enemy's ability to find, fix, and target us with their integrated air defense systems. Knowing the capabilities of the enemy's radars, weapons, and interoperability, I planned a path through the terrain designed to evade the enemy in the air and on the ground. In case the weather wouldn't allow low-altitude flying, I also planned a backup route to minimize our risk while flying at a higher altitude.

Once the route was set, I selected a final ingress route to the target using a prominent, easy-to-see geographical point to help guide the flight team to our objective. I chose the best weapon for destroying the target and planned an attack profile.

To sight the target and safely deliver the bombs, a fly-up maneuver was necessary. This part of the planning took the most amount of effort because the goal was to maximize our chances of seeing and killing the target while minimizing our exposure to any enemy threat. A weather backup plan was also established in case we could not visually see the target and had to fly in high above the terrain and weather. Navigation charts, satellite imagery, weapon ballistic parameters, threat engagement zones, and flight lineup cards all had to be produced for the team to use during the mission.

With all this in hand, I needed to put together a clear and concise briefing for my team so I could gain their commitment to our game plan. A couple hours before takeoff, the flight members would gather in a room to hear my detailed mission brief. We would discuss each phase of the flight: takeoff, rejoin, ingress/egress of the target area, and landing. Wingmen were briefed on their prioritized responsibilities to ensure the attainment of our objectives. Each conceivable contingency was briefed so everyone knew what to do—even if we lost sight or communication with each other.

After the briefing, we'd check our aircraft and weapons settings, then take off to meet our predetermined time over the target. Along the way, numerous obstacles—weather, systems malfunctions, threats—would require me to make split-second decisions to change the plan and reset my wingmen's various responsibilities.

Many times, our missions included airborne "aggressors" that flew utilizing Soviet formations, tactics, and weapons employment simulation to engage us in the air. Ground threat simulators, like surface-to-air missile (SAM) and anti-aircraft artillery (AAA) systems were included to provide more realistic training, which always made the missions more difficult and demanding. Whenever a contingency arose, I'd have to communicate clear, concise instructions so everyone would understand and commit to the new plan with our same mission objectives—while we're all flying at six hundred miles per hour and a couple hundred feet above the ground.

Watching and listening to one of these "battles" on a large screen that depicted our aircraft and the threats was quite a show. When enemy aircraft jumped our flight and we all reacted to defeat, neutralize, and engage the threat, the battles usually looked like total chaos, with aircraft all over the sky flying in different directions. After the threat was engaged, the screen would show our flight rejoin and continue toward our objective. The exhilaration of fighting our way to a target, popping up to find it and destroy it, and then fighting our way back home was something I'll never forget.

However, after landing, the flight was far from over.

The team would review videotapes from their aircraft that had recorded the entire mission, then gather in the briefing room to go over every phase of the mission. Every tape was played simultaneously to determine if everyone had fulfilled their responsibilities, delivered their ordinance within prescribed parameters, and survived the threats. We left no rock unturned. Many times, the debrief would last longer than the flight itself.

Any breaches of discipline or deviations from executing the plan—especially resulting in the simulated loss of one of our flight members—incurred a deep dive into why it happened and a compelling lesson learned for the next time around. Consequently, every mission developed our team into a more experienced fighting unit. The airmen could see for themselves that the more disciplined and committed we were to the plan, the higher our chance to kill and survive. And, as the team's experience grew over many years of flying together, the ability to flex to changing plans became instinctive and, I firmly believe, made us into the best Air Force in the world.

Later in my career, and as a direct result of Desert Storm, low-level flying became almost obsolete due to the improved technology of SAM and AAA systems. But, the "near rocks, far rocks" concept remains my most valuable planning tool for completing all short- and long-term tasks. Commitment to this tried-and-tested concept has become a way of life and the foundation for *all* of my daily processes.

I was trained to establish a list of both present and future priorities, as well as a cadence for every task at hand. Ultimately, "near rocks, far rocks" showed me how I should devote my energies to maximize my time, effort, and performance. I also used the concept as a leadership tool to develop objectives, prioritize tasks, assign responsibilities, and ensure attainment of goals with my team.

Just as flying a low-level mission required extensive planning and precision execution, so too does leading a team. The leader must first know where the team is going and how to get there. This means a well-thought-out plan with specific objectives and timelines must be developed and clearly communicated to every member. A leader must include his teammates in the process to develop buy-in and ownership of the plan. Good leaders must identify the critical, near-term tasks for their particular endeavors and must then crosscheck these priorities in a deliberate cadence to ensure the continued success of the team's objectives.

These high-priority tasks, objectives, and decisions must be concentrated on continuously and successfully completed so the team doesn't crash and burn. With the team's eye on the critical tasks, the leader can look beyond the horizon to formulate a new or improved vision for the team to commit to.

With the establishment of tasks, goals, and timelines, a unit can evaluate the progress of short- and long-term objectives, make course corrections, and provide valuable feedback on goal achievement. A host of group dynamics develops from this leadership style, including the delegation of responsibility to the lowest echelon, a synergy of effort, constructive feedback, and continuous improvement.

The importance of constant evaluation can't be overstated. This is the lifeblood of accountability and the foundation for building tomorrow's leaders. A concerted emphasis on attention to detail, daily excellence, and team over self becomes contagious and will permeate all levels of the organization. All of these individual and group dynamics, cultivated by the leadership, will build a culture of commitment that makes the sum of the whole greater than its parts. No obstacle or adversity can stop a team committed to the mission.

Flying low and fast was not only exhilarating as a youngster; it continues to profoundly affect my commitment to my flight through life. The adage I've shared has served me well in the cockpit and in the rush of life.

If you're searching for a path that will guide you and your team through any obstacle, you know what to tell them: "Near rocks, far rocks!"

TAKEAWAYS

- Committed leaders develop a clear path to their team's goals.
- Committed leaders seek input and buy-in from their team.
- Committed leaders constantly evaluate their team and themselves.

CHAPTER 2

EXEMPLARY DEDICATION
TO DUTY

TOM "HONEZ" JONES

"Any individual desiring to hold the lofty mantle of professional can do so, regardless of circumstances or background." —Bill Wiersma

---

WHEN SHE WAS JUST forty-two years old, my mother was diagnosed with cancer. To fight for her survival, she would undergo surgery and endure two years of chemotherapy.

Blessedly, she would win her battle.

When I once asked her what had gotten her through so many tough, demanding days, she simply remarked, "I committed myself to helping you boys grow up and have families of your own."

I'm glad she did. I know I wouldn't be the man I am today without her influence on my life. My mother remains the single greatest example of personal commitment I've ever witnessed.

Her strong-willed dedication to a cause is a fitting illustration for the kind of deep commitment I would witness, time and again, by female service members over the course of my military career.

I left my parents' household and entered the Air Force Academy in 1976—the same year that women were first allowed to attend service academies. Sixteen hundred airmen were inducted. One hundred and fifty were women. Sixty female airmen did not make it to graduation. Had I faced the kind of pressure and harassment they endured, I likely wouldn't have graduated either.

Back then, the Air Force officer corps was overwhelmingly male. We needed to increase the number of our female officers in order for our branch to reach its highest potential. But, collectively, we sure didn't make it easy on them.

In addition to the academic rigor required of Academy students, plus the daunting physical requirements and the emotional toll that accompanied daily Academy life, my female classmates constantly endured gender-based harassment in our boys' club—something I'm not proud to write, but that was the truth of the time. The overwhelming majority of cadets in the classes that had preceded mine—and even some in my own class—had made it abundantly clear that women were *not* welcome in *their* Academy.

However, the fact that ninety-seven female cadets graduated from that 1976 class, despite four long years of hostile treatment, is a testament to their fierce commitment and love of service.

In other words, they battled the cancer of sexism with their commitment to the Air Force and to each other.

Upon graduation, their military specialties ran the spectrum from pilots to battle managers to maintenance and personnel officers. Of those ninety-seven women, multiple became general officers. One achieved four-star rank. Today, the Air Force boasts more than thirty female general officers. I've known quite a few of them. Not all are Academy graduates, but their stories are remarkably (and damnably) similar: they all endured systemic organizational resistance based solely on their gender.

However, these accomplished airmen—an ironic term, I know—served as tremendous leaders and role models for our entire force, and particularly for those who joined the force after them. Airmen of all ranks benefitted from seeing women at the respective tops of their organizations. Furthermore, their service helped break down discriminatory beliefs and behaviors that had once dominated our service.

Nowhere was this more evident than in the male-dominated world of fighter aircraft. Although females had been allowed to fly aircraft in the Air Force since 1976, they were not allowed to fly fighters—and thus participate in combat—until 1993.

Yes. That's a seventeen-year gap.

Until 1993, fighter squadrons were definitely a boys-only club. (Think *Top Gun*.) We were elite groups of sky warriors, as close as brothers. When the possibility of women serving alongside us came up, I witnessed firsthand how the Air Force struggled to accept that such a change could happen. But the fierce debate ended when Congress decided that women could fly in combat. After that, it was leadership's responsibility to enact their new measures.

And I just so happened to be part of that leadership.

I felt the immense responsibility of ensuring that these women were provided every opportunity to succeed and to do so in an environment free from harassment and discrimination. Having watched my Academy classmates perform remarkably well when facing similar resistance more than twenty years earlier, I knew that the committed women who would become our teammates in the air would likewise rise to the challenge—especially if I could do my part to see that our organization judged them no differently based on their sex.

In 1993, I heard all the same complaints I'd heard in the late seventies:

- "This is a warrior society. It's no place for women."
- "Including women in our ranks will make us softer."
- "This means we'll have to lower our standards."

To all of these complaints, I wanted to reply, "But have you actually *met* these women?"

Including women in the Air Force and as combat fighters didn't make us less lethal; it made us more so. We benefitted from having teammates committed to the same exacting standards and lofty objectives required of us all. I couldn't understand why we'd said no for so long to having additional talented pilots—who happened to be women—who wanted to serve their country in the highest way possible. All we had to do was level the playing field so they could prove themselves by their merits, not their appearance.

Some were great fighter pilots; some were average; some needed extra attention—just like their male counterparts. And although the sample size is small—women comprise roughly 6 percent of Air Force pilots—every female fighter pilot I've met has an exceptional commitment to succeed and a unique perspective that has only added value to their respective organizations. The squadrons, groups, and wings I served in and commanded were definitively better because of their inclusion.

We were the world's greatest air force in 1976; we remain so today. I am convinced that's in part because we finally allowed females to join our ranks and fly in combat alongside us. In that time, we've witnessed numerous instances of female fighter pilots performing heroic actions under demanding conditions. Read about USAF Captain Kim Campbell in my chapter on courage, or search online for Southwest Airlines Captain Tammie Jo Shults, who was one of the first female fighter pilots in the Navy. These two women are just two examples of why our force is greater now than it was before 1976.

As a country, we still have work to do to ensure that women are given the same rights and the same access that men are granted. But I know this to be true: when women put their minds to something—when they commit to sticking around for their sons' sakes or to being willing to die for their country—they mean it and they will accomplish it.

Now, if only we can commit to doing what's right by them, the world will be a much better place.

TAKEAWAYS

- Committed leaders willingly face persecution for a greater cause.
- Committed leaders fight for their rightful positions as leaders.
- Committed leaders accomplish their missions.

CHAPTER 3

COMMITMENT AT 70,000 FEET

H. D. "JAKE" POLUMBO

"Desire is the key to motivation, but it's determination and commitment to an unrelenting pursuit of your goal—a commitment to excellence—that will enable you to attain the success you seek." —Mario Andretti

---

IMAGINE the worst you've ever felt when you've had the flu. The muscle aches. The foggy head. The weariness. The feeling that you'll never feel better again. The feeling that you might die. Keep those feelings in mind as you read about one of the most committed pilots I've ever flown with.

In March of 2009, Heather Fox was a captain in the United States Air Force under my command in the 380th Air Expeditionary Wing. We were stationed at Al Dhafra Air Base, located just outside of Abu Dhabi in the United Arab Emirates.

Throughout the history of the U-2 program, she was one of only eight female U-2 pilots in the USAF. That was accolade enough for me to trust her capabilities, but I'd known Captain Fox before our time together at Al Dhafra.

She'd previously flown with me as a T-38 instructor pilot at Sheppard Air Force Base when I'd been commander of the Euro-NATO Joint Jet Pilot Training Program in Wichita Falls, Texas. She had also worked for me when I was commander of the 9th Reconnaissance Wing at Beale Air Force Base in California, home of the U-2S Dragon Lady. (History buffs and USAF members might know the U-2 as the American spy plane piloted by Gary Powers that, while flying over eastern Europe on a reconnaissance mission, was shot down by the Soviets during the Cold War in 1960.)

Captain Fox was one of my terrific U-2 pilots in the wing at Al Dhafra, a base that had once gone unacknowledged by both the Americans and the Emiratis despite our huge US presence at the airfield. (Today, the sprawling base located an hour away from Dubai houses the Emirati Air Force's best fighters, the Lockheed Martin F-16 Block 60s.)

From previous experience in Texas and California, I knew that Captain Fox always conducted herself as a professional and was a terrific aviator and instructor. During our deployed time together, she had proven herself to be a brave leader in the squadron who could handle the toughest reconnaissance missions in any area in which we flew, whether that was Iraq, Afghanistan, or near the Horn of Africa, i.e., the easternmost tip of Africa that includes Somalia, Djibouti, Eritrea, and Ethiopia. This oftentimes violent section of the world was also the area of operations for the longest U-2 missions originating from this airbase.

I knew Captain Fox was good. It wasn't until one memorable mission in 2009—and memorable for almost all the wrong reasons—that I discovered how brave and committed she actually was.

I woke up on the day of that particular mission with an uneasy thought: *I don't feel well. I may have to get a replacement pilot to fly my mission.*

At the time, I was in the rotation as a U-2 pilot for a surveillance mission over Afghanistan. We had been tasked with gathering information on the Taliban and other notables within the country that both the US and NATO needed to learn more about. Secondarily, we were also asked to keep track of possible threats that could emanate from outside of Afghanistan, particularly in Iran. Such problems would often become readily apparent during our high-altitude flights.

The mission would likely last between nine and ten hours that day. As any trained U-2 pilot would do, I controlled my diet and sleep over the prior two days, knowing what challenges lay ahead for this particular mission. But, sometimes, even the best planning can't prepare the human body for a high-altitude flight. On the day of the mission, I woke up with an uneasy feeling in my bowels that I may not be able to fly the entire mission without experiencing some kind of difficulty. As I drove to work, I felt sure I'd need to hand off the mission.

Once on the flight line, naively believing that the possibility still existed that I could just get over whatever was ailing me, I began my normal pre-flight prep. But it became quickly apparent that I could not continue. I told the squadron commander and my backup pilot about my problems and that I would need to be replaced for this mission.

The awkwardness of the situation was more pronounced by the fact that I was the air expeditionary wing commander and a general officer. But I was also human, and my backup pilot—Captain Heather Fox—saw that. When I told her she would need to fly the mission that day, she gave me a relieved look since she'd already asked me twice, "How are you doing, sir? You feeling OK?" She hadn't meant it as a nicety; she had been legitimately concerned for my health since I didn't look well that morning.

When I asked if she was ready and willing, she immediately replied, "Sure." As the designated "mobile pilot," she was my backup for emergencies just like this. Because she would have been on my radio channel for the duration of the mission, she'd prepared physiologically in the same ways I had. She had also physically and mentally prepared herself should she be required to fly that day.

But I don't think she had prepared herself for the day she was about to have.

With a committed look in her eyes, Captain Fox immediately got to work. She took over mission preparation and studied the map and her objectives. She was checked out by supervisors and medical technicians to ensure her status and health were flight-ready. She carefully put on her pressurized flight suit, integrated into the U-2, took off, and then flew off toward Afghanistan, a two-and-a-half-hour flight just to get to her first objective.

Little did I know that Captain Fox's health wasn't as good as it had appeared to be in the flight briefing room.

She'd had a head cold a week prior to this mission. In fact, she'd just gone to see a flight surgeon two days prior for a checkup, telling the specially trained doctor that she was finally feeling better. She was placed back on flight status the next day and was qualified to be my mobile pilot and ultimately serve as my backup for this particular mission.

But flying at high altitudes for hours on end can make even a healthy person feel weak and disoriented.

Remember your worst flu?

Partway through the mission, after an uneventful flight to her reconnaissance area, Captain Fox began to feel the ill effects of high-altitude flying: fatigue, muscle stiffness, and joint pain. I had experienced some of these during my previous missions, but not all at once. As all high-altitude pilots know, the effects only become worse the longer you're in flight. I'm sure Captain Fox increased the pressure in her suit to try to counterbalance the effects, but it was to no avail. She was hurting, and she knew that flying in this state for a prolonged amount of time could do serious damage to her body—if not worse.

She began to experience decompression sickness and reported to mission control back in the states that she'd have to return to base immediately. The only problem was that she was three and a half hours away from base.

She struggled all the way back to the base, feeling increasingly worse the longer she flew. Heather relayed to me afterward that, while the flu symptoms were bad enough, the "really alarming parts were struggling to stay conscious on a turbulent day where the autopilot kept kicking off, and a rapid heartbeat that seemed like it was going to turn into a heart attack."

While the flight back to the UAE was difficult enough, it wasn't the most challenging part. Landing a U-2 after a long mission is hard enough for a person in good health. It's exponentially more difficult when your body and mind seem to be fighting against you.

Yet Captain Fox fought through this daunting physiological event. She arrived safely back at the base and successfully landed the $250-million airplane.

She revealed her professionalism, her dedication, and her

adept aviation skills in that return flight home. Even though she had "aborted" the mission in Afghanistan, she had succeeded in showing what it means to have bravery, courage, and *commitment* from start to mission finish.

In some instances, decompression sickness can't be diagnosed in the moment. Tests are later run to see if the pilot suffers from the effects of DCS or just its precursor feelings. Captain Fox had, indeed, suffered DCS in flight.

She recalls the nightmare scenario: "Turns out, there was so much nitrogen bubbling through my heart it went into tachycardia to try and get more oxygen. Docs debated whether a bubble in the brain or heart was responsible for my fight to stay conscious. At its worst (halfway down the boulevard), I gave serious thought to ejection, as it didn't seem possible to make it back. I made myself a deal to make it to the Gulf, where a carrier group was sitting, as a better chance of survival than on the ground in Pakistan . . . . Then, once in the Gulf, I thought I could make it to Oman, so I wouldn't be in the water . . . from there, Dhafra seemed possible."

The mission she flew in my stead was her last U-2 mission for that deployment in the Middle East. She went back to the states for further medical attention, which ultimately prevented her from flying for the next couple of years. After her recovery, Captain Fox was reassigned to Beale where she flew the "Deuce" at high altitude again to see if she had any lingering effects from her DCS event in Afghanistan. She did, and this proved to be her last flight in the storied aircraft.

Her deep commitment to the mission in 2009 resulted in an unfortunate loss of flying opportunities for this talented aviator, but it was a decision I know she would still make again today.

In fact, Lieutenant Colonel Heather Fox just finished a command tour in the RQ-4 Global Hawk Squadron at a base in the Middle East. She remains a mission-qualified pilot in the Global Hawk today and was recently promoted to the rank of colonel, which is no surprise to this author.

If you're wondering how she could be mission-qualified in the Global Hawk, it's an unmanned, remotely piloted, high-altitude reconnaissance aircraft that flies up to thirteen thousand miles for thirty hours or more without refueling. The pilot can never suffer from decompression sickness during an RQ-4 mission!

When I consider commitment to the mission, I see Captain Heather Fox, fighting against the worst flu-like symptoms she's ever experienced, landing a plane she loved to fly, and coming back strong to continue serving her country.

Real leaders always understand the commitment required to get the toughest job done.

TAKEAWAYS

- Committed leaders meet challenges—and danger —head on.
- Committed leaders endure setbacks and suffering for mission success.
- Committed leaders see obstacles as just challenges to overcome.

CHAPTER 4

LEADERSHIP IS A 24/7, FULL-CONTACT SPORT

JAMES "REV" JONES

"Individual commitment to a group effort—that is what makes a team work, a company work, a society work, a civilization work." —Vince Lombardi

---

OUTSTANDING. Excellent. Satisfactory. Marginal. Unsatisfactory.

Our wing could have been given any one of those ratings for a major operational readiness inspection. Such inspections are driven by higher headquarters and determine whether our team is truly ready for its designated combat mission.

Typically, a wing would spend a year conducting exercises in preparation for this inspection. These exercises are intense, complicated, and time-consuming. Every member of the wing, from top to bottom, has to hone their skills for their specific tasks so that, *collectively,* the unit could meet the high standards established by our higher headquarters.

While each individual plays a significant role during the

inspections, the unit commander is charged with ensuring the wing is prepared to meet the combat taskings levied against the unit, and, as such, bears the ultimate responsibility if the unit fails to meet the expected standards.

While I had participated in numerous inspections throughout my career, this particular evaluation was my first as a wing commander, and the unit was unique in its construct—not only in terms of the aircraft assigned to the wing and the associated mission, but also in the fact it was the Air Force's only truly "blended" wing, comprised of active duty airmen and members of the Air National Guard working side by side, as opposed to the more traditional methodology of associate units sharing the same equipment.

In addition to the legal differences (e.g., the Air National Guard reports to the governor through the adjutant general, unless called into active duty), we also needed to work our way through significant organizational issues. As the first active duty commander of this unit, which was administratively owned by the Air National Guard, there was a steep learning curve on my part associated with determining the processes and procedures to effectively manage the unit.

As this unit was the first and only unit of its kind, there were no established regulations or best practices to rely upon. The first commander of the unit, an Air National Guard general officer, did a spectacular job of putting the foundations for success in place, but there was still work to be done. Refining our processes and procedures while concurrently supporting combat operations in the Middle East was a full-time job, but we also had other major tasks that needed to be addressed. As we were in the midst of refining these processes and procedures, the schedule called for an operational readiness inspection—whether we were ready for it or not.

In a commander's perfect world, they will walk their organization through a series of training exercises leading up to the inspection. Unfortunately, when I took command, the organization had *just finished* their last preparatory training exercise. As such, I didn't have the chance to conduct a full-scale dress rehearsal with them. Therefore, my only opportunity to assess the wing came secondhand.

While I was unable to participate in the final exercise, I was able to take the out-brief and get a feel for our readiness to pass the inspection. While the unit had been working hard, it appeared that we weren't quite ready for the inspection, which was not surprising due to the demanding pace they were keeping to meet our combat commitments, which limited our ability to completely focus on the inspection preparations. And we still hadn't completely refined our daily operating procedures for in-garrison operations.

The team that had conducted and monitored the training exercises debriefed me on the dress-rehearsal exercise and their assessment of our team's readiness. At the end of their brief, we had two options. We could give the wing an internal rating of "satisfactory" while noting a number of deficiencies that fell short of the mark in an effort to provide a certain level of confidence going into the inspection. Alternatively, we could play the hand straight up and give the wing a "marginal" rating to reinforce that we still had plenty of work to do prior to the arrival of the inspection team.

After due consideration, I chose the latter. Our team immediately went to work to develop a plan to bring our performance up to expected standards in the few months we had remaining.

The first task at hand was to clearly communicate to everyone in the wing that the marginal rating in no way reflected on them as professional airmen. The blended wing had been running at full speed since the inception of the organization, trying to meet the myriad of tasks that kept coming their way. Our leadership team had to pull together and create the conditions that gave our airmen the time and resources they needed to be successful. We also had to commit ourselves—to one another, to the team, and to the mission.

I pulled our leadership team together to determine how best to proceed. We didn't have time to conduct another full-scale rehearsal, so we charted out each task we knew we still had to get better at. These tasks were broken down to the smallest organizational level that made sense, from the squadron on down to particular individuals. Most importantly, we empowered our subordinate formal and informal leaders to lead their respective groups through these tasks as they saw fit.

Within our day-to-day business, these leaders figured out the right timing and tempo to train their units. They also held their men and women accountable for raising the level of the organization to where we needed it to be by the time the inspection rolled around.

As if there wasn't enough pressure on us, my brother was the inspector general of the major command that my wing was aligned to. In other words, *my brother* would actually be the one in charge of bringing in the team who would evaluate *our* wing's capability to meet the operational requirements levied against us.

As we talked in the weeks leading up to the inspection, it became evident that our relationship posed potential challenges other units didn't have to face. Ultimately, we decided it was best if he didn't accompany the team on the inspection because, if we did well (which we certainly planned to do), we ran the risk of people thinking the inspection was biased due to our relationship. Alternatively, if we did poorly, there was a good chance Mom wouldn't let Tom come home for Christmas. It was the perfect example of discretion being the better part of valor.

The few months we had to prepare for the inspection went by in a flash. However, as I walked around the wing and observed their training activities, it became clear that they were motivated and fully committed to excelling during the inspection. As each day passed, our confidence increased, and it became apparent the wing would pull it all together in time—but just in time.

No doubt: the inspection was tough.

They gave our team a demanding set of requirements, from generating airplanes to deploy within a challenging timeline, simulating a deployment to an austere location, then setting up operations and conducting simulated combat missions in the toughest of conditions, including operating within simulated environments resulting from an adversary's use of weapons of mass destruction.

At the end of a long five days, the evaluation team handed us our rating: excellent.

I couldn't have been prouder of our team.

To move from marginal to excellent in the span of three months was a testament to the undeterred commitment to succeed held by everyone within the organization. Our rating proved what could be done when people approach even a single task with full commitment every day. Our collective success showed how a team could overcome a seemingly insurmountable task. Our newfound confidence revealed what I knew our wing could always achieve: excellence in all we do.

To be perfectly clear, this success was not *my* success by any means. Rather, our success could be traced back to the formal and informal leaders throughout the subordinate organizations. They challenged their people, laid out an executable path, encouraged them to take risks, and helped them train while still attending to their day-to-day duties.

When we were awarded an excellent rating, the entire wing walked out of that debrief with their heads held high. They knew they had accomplished a significant feat. In fact, I believe that moment may have been a turning point for our wing. After that inspection, no task felt too heavy for our team. No pressure was too great. Whether they had to tackle a task related to combat, training, or even administration, they approached each task with the same level of commitment they'd shown in those three months leading up to our inspection.

And they received excellent results every time.

I learned many lessons through that experience: Leadership is a 24/7 job. It does not relent, especially in the military.

Leadership must also happen within all levels of an organization to be effective. Had the leaders of each of the subordinate organizations not have been capable or committed, we collectively would have failed.

And leadership is often its own reward. Few things in life are as gratifying than successfully leading a team through challenging times—especially when you can build a leadership team that helps carry the load each and every day.

I went on to a number of assignments after leaving that particular wing, but I'm still grateful for the opportunity to

work with and alongside the *excellent* men and women in the
116th Air Control Wing.

TAKEAWAYS

- Committed leaders pledge themselves to the tasks
  at hand every single day.
- Committed leaders seek out the toughest
  challenges to solve versus avoiding them.
- Committed leaders' commitment to the success of
  the unit is visible and contagious.

CHAPTER 5

A HIGHER CALLING

RICHARD "BEEF" HADDAD

"A man who won't die for something is not fit to live."
—Martin Luther King Jr.

I GREW UP IN KEARNY, Arizona, a small copper-mining community where my highest aspirations should have been landing a job at the copper mine, earning enough to buy a brand-new pickup, marrying a local girl, and raising kids to follow in my copper-toned footsteps.

But, thankfully, that's not what my father wanted. As an entrepreneur and the owner of his own clothing store, as well as a three-decade justice of the peace, he wanted more for his children. I wanted more too.

Like many small-town high school athletes, I thought my ability on the football field could carry me away from Kearny. I thought I was a pretty good offensive and defensive lineman. In fact, I assumed I'd be a state standout. But my senior year didn't turn out as well as I'd hoped. Still, I dreamed. I had a burning desire to play D-I football for some powerhouse.

During my senior year, I received a few requests from some small four-year colleges and a few junior colleges, but I wasn't interested in playing for such comparatively low-level colleges. I wanted the thrill and the challenge—and, let's be honest—the respect of playing for a Division I school.

That changed when I received a recruiting letter that would forever alter the trajectory of my life. The United States Air Force Academy outside of Colorado Springs, Colorado, wanted me to apply.

At the time, I had no interest in joining the military. Even though my father had served in the Navy during World War II and the Army during the Korean War, he'd never really spoken about his time in service. And even though I'd taken part in my high school's Junior ROTC program and had liked the staff, I'd never taken to the regimentation and everything else that accompanies a group revolving around the Marine Corps.

So the USAF letter was a surprise. Plus, it was my only offer from a D-I school. I took weeks to ponder whether I'd apply. Figuring it would be my only chance to achieve my dream while also receiving a stellar education, I applied.

I was rejected. Sort of.

My SAT scores on the English section hadn't been high enough to meet their entrance criteria. However, the admissions officers at the Academy must have seen my potential, either in my athletic ability, my academic ability, or something else. They offered to accept me into the USAF Academy Preparatory School, which is located on the same campus as the main Academy.

I readily accepted, and, even though it would become one of the more challenging years of my life, it was one of the best decisions of my life too.

The prep school was exactly what I needed to bridge the gap between my small-town life and moving into a D-I school. The school only had two hundred or so students. We took English and math classes, as well as periodic SAT exams to see if we were progressing well. I often felt lacking compared to my classmates, many of whom had been granted the opportunity to take advanced-level courses at their high schools that just weren't offered at mine. Overcoming my academic deficiencies was an incredible struggle for me at this time. But I committed myself to becoming a better student, knowing that the goal ahead of me was worth the cost before me.

On top of my studies, I was also playing football. One reason I agreed to attend the preparatory school was that I'd still be able to play D-I football. We may have been playing nearby college JV teams, but I was still playing at the collegiate level. Best of all, I would still be eligible to play all four years once I was in the Academy. I committed myself to becoming a better football player, knowing that playing for the Academy would be much more challenging than playing for the prep school.

I studied hard, applied myself, and was able to raise my English score to an acceptable level. I was accepted into the Academy, where I then persevered for four years and was transformed into the man I am today.

I had the opportunity to play for three different head coaches, one of whom was Bill Parcells. I never started a game until my senior year, when I was finally placed in the starting lineup as an offensive lineman.

I loved the game—and I still do—but playing D-I collegiate-level football wasn't just a game, a hobby, or even a simple extracurricular activity. It was a job. In fact, at that time, when I was juggling an average of twenty-one credit hours every semester, playing football was my second job. However, succeeding in both aspects of my life back then required that I learn how to manage my time and seek assistance from my teachers.

To say that I survived those four years might be an understatement. I was often weary and would sometimes have doubts about what I was capable of achieving. But I always came back to the commitment I'd made to myself and, ultimately, to the school: to be a quality athlete and to receive a high-caliber education.

But something else happened during those four years.

I learned about the Air Force. I became an airman. Through the commitment I'd had to sports and athletics, I learned about the much deeper and longer-lasting commitment I'd ultimately make by swearing an oath to defend the Constitution of the United States against all enemies, foreign and domestic.

Really, the seeds for this change had been subtly planted about a week after my arrival at the prep school. Colonel Ben Pollard, a former POW who was commander of the school at the time, had assembled us all in the auditorium. He said, "Look to your right and look to your left."

Dozens of heads turned to look at each other.

He continued, "Only one out of three of you will be here in five years when it's time to graduate from the Air Force Academy."

In essence, he questioned our commitment up front

because he knew how grueling the next few years of our lives could be.

The two men I sat next to that day would become my good friends over our years at the Academy. All three of us graduated. And all these decades later, we are still best friends. I know each of these men to be committed to our country still today, as am I—all because we were first committed to just making it through school and to playing D-I football.

The Academy knew how to raise our sights and shift our commitments from that of boys to that of men, from the pursuits of youth in academics and athletics to the pursuits of airmen in leadership and service.

However, during my long military career, I did eventually marry the woman of my dreams, raise a family, and buy that new pickup.

TAKEAWAYS

- Committed leaders show commitment in all things, from the minor to the major.
- Committed leaders push through hardships.
- Committed leaders commit to something beyond themselves.

PART 2

COURAGE

CHAPTER 6

THE RISK OF COURAGE

RICHARD "BEEF" HADDAD

"I learned that courage was not the absence of fear, but the triumph over it. The brave man is not he who does not feel afraid, but he who conquers that fear." — Nelson Mandela

---

THE NEED for courage isn't limited to military combat. At certain points in any person's life, we're all asked to show strength of mind to carry on despite danger or difficulty, or to overcome fear in the face of grave risk.

I think back to my Lebanese ancestors on my father's side, who I'm told immigrated to the US around 1912. After their arrival at Ellis Island, they eventually found their way west, to Arizona, which wasn't even a state until that year. One man from their village of Baskinta had settled there; the rest of their village apparently followed. To earn a living, they sold clothes from the trunks of their cars to area miners. Later, my father became a Justice of the Peace, as well as a successful entrepreneur.

Even as a child, I was impressed by the stories I was told. Despite not being able to speak English and the bias they likely faced in those early days—especially so far west—my ancestors risked severe adversity for an opportunity to better their lives for themselves and their children.

I'm a grateful recipient of the courage they showed a century ago. Because of their sacrifices, I was ultimately able to attend the Air Force Academy, be commissioned, and rise to the rank of major general.

During my time in service, I experienced hundreds of more instances of courage under fire—literally. But during two wartime deployments, I witnessed the courage of our airmen rise to the forefront, even as their lives hung in the balance.

In 1988, after leaving active duty, I joined the Reserve at the 711th Special Operations Squadron, flying AC-130 gunships. Two years later, we engaged Iraqi troops under Saddam Hussein in Operation Desert Storm.

Our unit was not immediately called up, but I wanted to be a part of it, so I volunteered to join a Milwaukee C-130 unit to work tactics and current operations during Operation Desert Shield, a ground job based in Sharjah in the United Arab Emirates. After a month, I returned to the states with a better understanding of the war. I didn't expect my AC-130 unit to be called for duty—until we were called for duty.

Even more surprising, young Captain Haddad would be leading the five aircraft heading to Iraq.

To make it more challenging, the men within my reserve unit had never been deployed to combat (with the exception of a few Vietnam veterans). They had either been reservists from Day One or they had left active duty and joined the Reserves. Consequently, my men were well-trained but green. By the time we'd left the states, each one of them had had to deal with leaving their family, friends, and civilian jobs behind in order to fly into a combat zone.

A-model gunships can't carry a lot of external fuel, so flying from the states to the Middle East required multiple stops. On one layover in Sigonella, Italy, many of the men called home and heard that an H-model active-duty gunship, Spirit 03, had been shot down the day before with the loss of the entire fourteen-man crew.

Many of their wives had been panicked and crying on the phone. Few had previously been through a combat deployment with their husbands. Many couples had not even been married when the husband was originally on active duty. Later, they would band together and support each other, but we couldn't know that then.

Talk about a morale-killer.

I believe that was the first time many of those airmen realized both the challenge and the importance of their service—it became real for them. Seeing the looks on their faces, I tried to keep them motivated, instilling as best I could that our mission was our job, risks be damned. We had to perform our mission, whatever it might be, because our ground forces and our country would be relying on us.

Upon arrival, we were alerted that our unit would not be conducting any daylight reconnaissance since Spirit 03 had been shot down returning after dawn from a night mission. Instead, our assignment would be nighttime reconnaissance along the Iraq–Kuwait border. When the ground war began, three of our aircraft would rotate into and out of the prescribed orbit area. Once Aircraft One had used its fuel, Aircraft Two would take its place. Once Aircraft Two had used its fuel, Aircraft Three would take its place. Thus, our presence in the sky protecting our ground troops would remain constant.

On the night of this particular engagement, I was in command of Aircraft Two.

Aircraft One had been orbiting for a while and was getting close to its return fuel limit. However, our air weapons controller directed them to a kill zone north of the Iraq–Kuwait border. I can only imagine what my men were thinking as Aircraft One was the first plane to be cleared into a combat zone since the H-model gunship had been shot down. At this point, the Iraqis were hightailing it out of Kuwait City and heading back home to Iraq. Aircraft One engaged in what was effectively a "turkey shoot" on these fleeing enemies: a caravan of tanks, trucks, busses, weapon platforms, and armored personnel carriers. Still, their copilot relayed that I needed to hurry up and relieve them.

I did. With nearly a full load of fuel and ample ammunition, we quickly arrived and proceeded to pound targets along The Highway of Death, which is what we'd eventually call the road from Kuwait City to Iraq because so many Iraqi military had fled Kuwait on that road and had been killed in the process. The Iraqi Army couldn't be allowed to return to Baghdad and regroup.

As we continued to do our job, our electronic warfare officer began picking up signals that anti-aircraft weapons had been set up. We'd stirred the hornet's nest, and the hornets were about to fight back.

At what seemed like the same moment, our engineer alerted us that our fuel level had dropped to the point where we needed to return. However, as we rolled out, our fuel level returned to normal. Immediately, our engineer said we could stay and continue the fight.

I thought, *How surprising that these men, with that fatal H-model crash in their minds, want to remain in combat. Their training and professionalism have kicked in. They're so engrossed in the mission they don't want to leave.*

But I knew we'd done enough damage. It was time for us to roll out, regardless of our fuel level. On our way out, the Iraqis gave us a parting shot: they launched a surface-to-air missile at us. Fortunately, it wasn't accurate and didn't come close to hitting us. But the men were exhilarated by that night's events. So was I. But, more than anything else, I was profoundly impressed by their steadfast courage under fire.

By the time Aircraft Three relieved us, the Iraqis had set up enough weapons, and our third gunship could only make one or two low-level orbits before having to roll out. Gratefully, my decision to depart had been the right one at the right time. Anytime you can take a crew into combat, complete your mission objective, and return home with all of your crew members is a good day.

That was a good day.

My final story of courage happened in the aftermath of 9/11, when so many thousands of us, both military personnel and civilians, had to show courage in the face of an unparalleled terrorist attack.

In October of 2001, I led a contingent of five airplanes and eight crews, comprised of both reservists and active duty airmen, into Afghanistan for our initial invasion. We were flying five M-130s, penetrating tankers that fly low to the ground to perform several special ops missions, including refueling helicopters using wing-based fueling pods and booms.

Our first missions were on targets in Operations "Gecko" and "Rhino," which have been related in open sources. On one mission, we had been commanded to provide fuel to the helicopter task force that would attack Gecko, the residential compound of Mullah Mohammed Omar, leader of the Taliban. I was mission commander, with five aircraft under my control, plus another aircraft in Pakistan that we would need to call in later that night.

For the larger mission, nothing went as planned.

Consequently, I became the puppet master of our rapidly moving aircraft, ensuring that the Army's helos received fuel where they needed it and *not* where we had planned for the refueling to take place. Our nine-member crew, as well as the nine-member crews of my other five aircraft, performed spectacularly that night. They'd fly up to a KC-135 refueling aircraft, fill their fuel tanks, then fly down to the Army helos and refuel them. My team flew back and forth all night long—fifteen hours of nonstop flying in mountainous terrain and all via night-vision goggles. That mission had to have been the most tasking and difficult flying any of them had done.

But each airman understood the risks and the stakes. Their unrelenting determination to see the mission succeed displayed the kind of dogged courage I've seen time and again during my military service. In fact, their courage reminded me of my Lebanese ancestors, who likewise understood the risks and the stakes of their westward travel. Yet they moved forward.

In all three instances, I witnessed courage rise from the combination of vision, preparation, and overcoming fear. With vision, my ancestors saw a better life ahead and my crews saw "Mission accomplished!" before them.

With preparation, both my ancestors and my crews knew they could handle whatever was thrown at them because they'd either endured worse or had been trained to expect the worst.

And all of them overcame fear and showed their courage. To be honest, I felt fear during that Desert Storm operation and during our invasion of Afghanistan. But I also knew I had a job to do, and my crews knew they had to do their jobs. Consequently, we overcame our fears and accomplished our mission.

If "courage is doing what you're afraid to do," as Eddie Rickenbacker said, my family, myself, and my men displayed courage at its best.

TAKEAWAYS

- Courageous leaders see the goal ahead of the challenge.
- Courageous leaders are well prepared for any eventuality.
- Courageous leaders overcome fear.

CHAPTER 7

NO TIME TO FEAR

TOM "HONEZ" JONES

"I wish it were possible to pull all my thoughts on paper, those which run through my mind when I get in battle like we were today. It's so funny to say I'm not afraid. I don't have time to be afraid. I just try to shoot down an airplane without getting another one on my tail. My stomach and neck muscles are going to be strong by the time this war is over." — Major General (Ret) Charles Bond, USAF

THE WAY HOLLYWOOD depicts fighter pilots is rarely accurate. Those handsome heroes wear their uniforms wrong and their hair too long. They're often all men. And these movies often fail to adequately capture the true essence of life in the daily work of a military pilot.

And the dogfights?

Well, it's easy to be courageous when the stakes aren't real.

So let me tell you about three service members under my

leadership who epitomized real courage in the face of devastating stakes.

In 2003, I was the wing commander of the 332nd Air Expeditionary Wing at Al Jaber Air Base in Kuwait at the onset of Operation Iraqi Freedom. We were stationed about seventy-five miles south of the Iraqi border. My wing was comprised of fighters and support aircraft piloted by service members from across the total force, which meant the men and women who reported to me were from the Air Force, the Air Force Reserve, and the Air National Guard.

Consequently, I didn't know many of the airmen at Al Jaber—but I'll never forget Captain Kim Campbell.

During my thirty-five-year career, I witnessed countless examples of courage under multiple circumstances: in the air and on the ground, and under physical or emotional duress—or both. I also heard grandiose boasts from military personnel about their courageous actions, but the proof of their courage always resided in the verifiability of their actions. When it really counted, did their courage really reveal itself?

I grew up in a community and led my teams where hollow words weren't tolerated. Regardless of your skill-set or your rank, you were expected to be courageous—and you were often required to prove it.

Captain Campbell proved it.

On April 7, 2003, my battle staff alerted me that an A-10 jet in my wing had suffered heavy battle damage over Baghdad. The A-10's pilot, Captain Campbell, along with her squadron, had been supporting US ground forces in Baghdad. Their squadron had been conducting multiple passes below the clouds, firing rockets on enemy targets and strafing the area with their 30-mm cannons.

On Captain Campbell's last pass, her A-10 was struck by enemy fire.

The aircraft rolled left and began a nosedive. She quickly diagnosed that she'd lost hydraulics and switched to the emergency backup system. In other words, she was forced to fly manually. She steered the jet away from the enemy and toward friendly lines.

As she escaped, her flight lead notified her of just how extensive the damage was. She had massive holes in her ailerons and rudders, a.k.a. flight control surfaces, as well as in the aircraft fuselage, likely caused by anti-aircraft artillery and/or shoulder-fired missiles. Plus, to make matters worse and much more time-sensitive, her jet was streaming fluids.

Captain Campbell fought her jet to maintain control for the roughly forty-minute return to base. To fly an A-10 weighing approximately thirty thousand pounds *without* hydraulic assistance is similar to driving a car without power steering. Every steering input, in every direction, is met with immediate and forceful resistance. In Captain Campbell's case, that resistance was caused by aerodynamic forces. Yet, somehow, despite the jet's extensive aerodynamic damage and her severe lack of flight controls, Captain Campbell maintained control of the jet and opted to fly back to the base instead of ejecting.

Later, I would have multiple experienced A-10 pilots tell me they would *never* have attempted what she did. They all said they were certain they wouldn't be able to keep control of the aircraft. I still don't know how she was able to fight that jet for that long under those circumstances.

Of course, flying a damaged aircraft is one thing. Landing it is another.

As her A-10 approached our base, I positioned my command vehicle near the runway, where Fire and Rescue personnel awaited her arrival. Because her jet had no hydraulics, she would have to land without normal landing gear functions, she'd have no braking capabilities, and she wouldn't be able to steer on rollout (i.e., after she'd landed the plane). In other words, it was anyone's guess as to where she'd end up. That is, if she could even get on the runway in the first place.

However, in a feat of remarkable airmanship, Captain Campbell landed the aircraft squarely in the center of the runway. She somehow steered that tattered aircraft with what little rudder authority she had left. Her A-10 rolled to a stop without having departed the controlled surface even once. In other words, if there's such a thing as a perfect landing for a severely damaged plane, she'd just achieved that.

As she shut the engines off and climbed down from the cockpit, we swarmed around her aircraft. She was obviously thankful to be safely on the ground. But it didn't seem like she was very emotional—until she saw the extent of the jet's damage with her own eyes. (In fact, we would have to write the A-10 off as a total loss.)

That's when she realized what an incredible feat she'd just accomplished.

She was granted a few days reprieve from flying duties, but she was back on the flying schedule within days.

When I later asked Captain Campbell about her thought process after the initial attack, she told me she'd never doubted she'd be able to return to base—nor did she doubt her ability to fly the aircraft.

Captain Campbell's courage under fire, combined with her great leadership qualities, make her a tremendous role model for women and men alike. Her story has been recounted many times, and she is modest when retelling it. But, the fact remains:

·

she displayed extraordinary physical courage, decision-making, leadership, and aviation skill in recovering her badly damaged aircraft.

When I think of courage, I see Captain Campbell's ailing A-10 coming in for a perfect landing.

I also see two enlisted weapons troops risking their safety—even their lives—to save their fellow service members.

About four weeks into the war in Iraq, I was awakened when the command post called me. "Sir, we have an incident on the flight line involving an A-10 and a smoking rocket pod." (In hindsight, I have to wonder why A-10s always seem to be involved.)

A dozen or more pilots, maintainers, fire crews, and others awaited me at the scene. They all pointed me toward the aircraft parked some distance away which was, sure enough, billowing white smoke from a partially emptied rocket pod mounted under its right wing.

The issue was compounded by our lack of space on base. Due to our sheer number of fighters, we were forced to park them wingtip to wingtip. Picture "Battleship Row" at Pearl Harbor. If the A-10's faulty rocket "cooked off," it would damage the aircraft in its vicinity.

Since some of those jets were also loaded with munitions, the cascading effect could be devastating.

I assessed our options. We couldn't tow the aircraft away with a hung rocket. The safety folks wanted to clear everyone away and just wait. Maintenance and ops wanted to solve the issue as soon as possible so we could continue generating sorties for combat. Clearly, there was no "book" answer for our predicament.

So, I asked for suggestions as to how we should handle the escalating situation.

After a few minutes, an enlisted weapons troop said, "Hell, sir, let me go grab a trailer and my tools. I'll download the whole pod, put it in the trailer, and haul it off to the other side of the runway. If it hasn't cooked off by now, I doubt it ever will."

Though loaded with danger, his idea was the best one I'd heard. I nodded my assent.

We supplied the courageous man and an assistant with protective gear and sent them toward the billowing white smoke. Fifteen minutes later, he'd accomplished just what he said he'd do. The two airmen hauled the smoking rocket and pod off the flight line, which allowed our combat operations to continue. The rocket, thankfully, never fully ignited.

That young man and his assistant knowingly placed themselves in personal danger to assure that our wing could continue combat operations.

And I don't remember a moment of hesitation from the man who'd made the suggestions. His calm attitude revealed his courageous confidence. I could tell what he was thinking: *I know what has to be done. Just authorize me to do it.* The courage and leadership he displayed were infectious. And his "get the job done" attitude on that flight line was never any higher than right after his actions aligned with his intentions.

To be a great leader, you must be willing to risk your personal (or professional) safety to achieve mission success. Additionally, your organization must view you as someone unfazed by precarious situations. Captain Campbell and those two brave rocket retrieval "specialists" epitomize that kind of courageous leadership.

Remember: you don't have to be in combat to be courageous—but you *do* have to be courageous to be a great leader.

TAKEAWAYS

- Courageous leaders prove themselves by their actions, not their words.
- Courageous leaders prove themselves when the fire is hottest.
- Courageous leaders know what has to be done— and then do it.

CHAPTER 8

THAT'S ALL WE KNOW. WHAT DO YOU WANT TO DO NOW?

JAMES "REV" JONES

"Success is not final, failure is not fatal: it is the courage to continue that counts." —Winston Churchill

---

AS THE DEPUTY combined forces air component commander for Air Forces Central Command from the summer of 2011 to the summer of 2012, I was responsible for managing the day-to-day execution of air operations in Central Command, with a primary focus on supporting campaigns in Afghanistan and Iraq.

Within a few months of arriving in theater, I was notified of the loss of a remotely piloted aircraft within the combat zone. This particular aircraft was part of a relatively small fleet and was valued at approximately $70 million. At the time, I was the senior officer in the operations center, which meant this problem was *my* problem.

We were able to track its flight path through radar feeds as it descended, so we had a general idea of where the crash site was located. We then directed other Intelligence, Surveillance, and Reconnaissance (ISR) assets to the area, which enabled us to locate the actual crash site relatively easily.

The question then became: So, now what?

Typically, the Air Force will launch an intensive formal investigative process when there is a mishap so they can determine the proximate causes that led to the incident with a sole focus on putting preventative measures into place to avert a reoccurrence.

As such, the standard process is always to try to recover as much of the wreckage as possible and to isolate the crash site to protect its integrity, similar to what police officers do at a crime scene. But it's a much more complicated process in a combat zone.

However, depending on the situation, e.g., amount of hostile activity, access to the site, ability to protect the convoy/recovery teams, it may still be prudent to try to recover as much of the wreckage as possible. In fact, there may be additional urgency to do so in order to prevent the enemy from exploiting any data that could be recovered from the site.

As such, a recovery effort was my initial inclination—but things quickly became more complicated.

Our ISR assets showed groups of the indigenous population being drawn to the site. Whether they were approaching out of curiosity, trying to find something of value to sell on the black market, or for any other purpose, their presence significantly changed the situation.

To keep them away from the site—not only due to concerns over exploitation but also for their safety—we directed a fighter aircraft to make multiple low passes over the crash site. This nonlethal show of force was marginally effective at first, but, within a short period of time, the people would quickly return to dig through the wreckage once again.

With the assets we had on-site, it was too difficult to discern whether the crowd was friendly or contained insurgents. Plus, recovery would require ground units to put together a hasty convoy plan to get there, secure the site, spend an extended period of time trying to recover as much of the wreckage as possible—and all in contested areas with potential IEDs. Then they'd have to run the same gauntlet to get home again.

In a perfect world, I would have had time to put together a team of experts to help work through all of the options, but this scenario was about as imperfect as it got.

Leadership in a benign environment, when everything is going well, can be relatively easy. In fact, if there is no need to adjust course or drive change, effective management may be more important than true leadership.

However, it becomes much more challenging when important decisions must be made that may have significant consequences. Under the best circumstances, there's time to work through a disciplined, concerted decision-making process where you can weigh all of the variables to come to an optimum decision. More often than not, you may be forced to make decisions that affect the organization with imperfect information due to exigencies of the situation, be it timelines, the need to react to rapidly shifting operating environments, or other similar drivers.

I was forced to make a decision with imperfect information.

I pulled the senior officers together in the Combined Air Operations Center, our primary command and control facility, did a quick huddle to get their thoughts, took a deep breath, and then directed a fighter aircraft to make multiple strafe runs and bomb passes to destroy the wreckage.

As we watched the action through the ISR feeds, I kept waiting for the phone to ring with questions from the Air Staff or Air Combat Command asking what the hell I was doing—but the phone never rang. In fact, no one in my chain of command questioned the call because they knew the circumstances required making the call with the information at hand. They trusted I would make a decision appropriate to the circumstance.

That moment was a perfect example of trusting those who work for you and empowering them to make the necessary calls as required, especially when there's not enough time for a more deliberate process.

Not long afterward, I realized the importance of trust once again when we were faced with a high-risk recovery mission to pick up a wounded soldier and transport him back to the closest medical treatment facility.

At the time, there was a significant sandstorm that had reduced visibility to the point that it required my approval for the recovery mission. The ops floor had been in contact with the "Pedros," the call sign of helicopter crews charged with conducting rescue missions. Their motto is "that others may live," and these heroes routinely and willingly put themselves at risk to recover wounded/isolated personnel, often in the most demanding of circumstances.

The alert crew was standing by to execute the mission. They just needed my approval. After a quick confirmation that the aircraft commander was willing to accept the mission and assurance that they would abort the mission if it appeared the weather would prevent successful execution, I told them to press on. Then I anxiously waited for mission results.

As I recall, within approximately thirty minutes, I received word that the crew had recovered the injured individual and had safely delivered him to the medical treatment facility. Mission fully accomplished.

I'll never forget the courage of that crew who unhesitatingly volunteered to take the mission—and I'm sure the person they picked up feels the same.

So, it may be more comfortable to study a problem from all possible angles before making a decision, but a "perfect" decision made late is tantamount to making no decision at all, which is ultimately a failure of leadership.

All you can do is make the best decision you can with the information that's available, hope for the best, and be ready to adjust course as required. You might not have the perfect solution, but you're at least moving in the right direction and giving positive direction to those who work for you.

They deserve no less.

TAKEAWAYS

- Courageous leaders must often make significant decisions based on imperfect information.
- Courageous leaders are willing to adapt to the circumstances at hand versus being overcome by them.
- Courageous leaders don't wait for the perfect answer; they seek positive forward momentum at all times.

CHAPTER 9

STAND FIRMLY

ROB "MUMBLES" POLUMBO

"The ultimate measure of a man is not where he stands in moments of comfort and convenience, but where he stands at times of challenge and controversy." —Martin Luther King, Jr.

WHAT WOULD you do if the government, your superiors, and the national media were pressuring you to act against your integrity?

In two separate events, that's effectively what happened to my boss, General Ronald Fogleman, the chief of staff of the Air Force from 1994–1997. I had the extreme privilege to work for him as his aide-de-camp beginning in 1996 through the final eighteen months of his career.

While I learned valuable lessons about the inner workings of the Department of Defense and how the military makes its way inside the Washington DC beltway, I gained much more insight about the courage necessary to lead. But the ways in which I learned them were difficult and tragic, for a host of reasons.

In 1996, with our forces deployed in support of Operation Southern Watch, a truck laden with tons of explosive chemicals was detonated just outside the living quarters of hundreds of US military personnel at Khobar Towers in Dhahran, Saudi Arabia.

In what would become known as the Khobar Towers bombing, the terrorist act killed nineteen American military personnel, wounded more than two hundred others, and harmed hundreds more Saudi soldiers and civilians.[1] Muslim extremists protesting US involvement in the Middle East had carried out the deadly and heinous attack.

A similar method of attack had previously occurred at Beirut in 1983 and Riyadh in 1995, but the Khobar attack had used a substantially larger bomb. It was estimated to have the power of over twenty thousand pounds of TNT—twice the power of the Beirut bomb and one hundred times the strength of the Riyadh explosion.

The secretary of defense immediately ordered an investigation on the attack led by General Wayne Downing, a retired four-star Army general. The comprehensive report listed twenty-six findings and over a hundred recommendations on improving our force protection, not only in the Middle East but also at locations across the globe. One of the findings alleged that the commander of the Khobar facility did not adequately protect his forces from a terrorist attack. This very serious charge set off numerous DoD follow-up investigations and legal processes to determine if dereliction of duty had occurred, which could be punishable under the Uniformed Code of Military Justice.

At the time of the attack, the base commander was Brigadier General Terryl Schwalier, a US Air Force officer. He was at the end of his one-year tour as the 4404th Provisional Wing commander. The Downing report concluded that Schwalier had not done enough to protect his base from a terrorist attack. As a result, he was found responsible for the loss of life and related casualties at Khobar Towers.

The secretary of the Air Force and my boss were directed by the secretary of defense to conduct an independent investigation to review all findings raised in the Downing report, including a disciplinary and court-martial review for actions and omissions by General Schwalier. The exhaustive, ninety-day investigation, led by General James Record, 12th Air Force commander, included dozens of interviews with Saudi officials, State Department and intelligence personnel, commanders in Schwalier's chain of command, and staff and members of his wing. Every decision he made over his one-year tour was chronicled and evaluated to determine if he had done everything in his authority to protect the base from the myriad of probable attacks assessed by then-current intelligence reports.

Record's team reviewed every Department of Defense and Air Force instruction (a.k.a. regulation), as well as the policies set by the commander of US Central Command relating to the force protection responsibilities of a base commander. Ultimately, the independent report refuted every derogatory finding that had been leveled against Schwalier in the Downing report. He had *not* been derelict in the performance of his duties.

The difference between Downing and Record's reports lay in how the two envisioned the situational awareness of Schwalier prior to the attack. Downing presumed Schwalier should have had perfect awareness of an impending attack and preemptively taken action to stop it. This 20/20 hindsight vantage point didn't take into account the ever-present fog of war, which Record believed impacted Schwalier's situational awareness and, ultimately, his decision-making processes. The findings and recommendations of both reports were briefed to my boss, who supported Record's investigation over Downing's.

With the upper echelon of our national command authority put on alert that our force protection posture was not up to speed—and still no one to blame for the death and injury of so many Americans—the DC beltway politics and media went looking for a target. This pressure influenced the secretary of defense to direct another look at Schwalier's actions to determine if administrative disciplinary measures should be taken against the officer.

The Air Force inspector general and judge advocate general completed the follow-on investigation. The results of the investigation supported Record's report and recommended no administrative action against Schwalier.

But this story didn't end there.

The pundits and media, fueled by inflammatory congressional hearings, wanted a scapegoat to blame for this attack. With mounting pressure—and a new secretary of defense in place—the investigation was reopened.

When this happened, I could tell my boss saw the writing on the wall. He knew that the likely outcome of this review from the new secretary of defense was to pin the blame on Schwalier, resulting in disciplinary action against the officer. This would be done to quell the media's pressure on the administration to hold someone accountable for these deaths.

But how fair is it to blame a man who did all he could in light of the significant limitations of insufficient support from the host nation, a lack of updated intelligence on terrorist plots, and unsuitable facilities centered in the middle of a city? Surely, someone would have the courage to stand up for him.

For those familiar with beltway politics, the rest of this story is nothing new.

The Department of Defense review sided with the original Downing report and concluded that Schwalier should have done *more* to prevent and mitigate this attack. To me, the findings seemed like a classic move to provide the administration cover from culpability for their inadequate coordination of military basing and force protection with Saudi Arabia. In addition, this decision was made to appease the press and the American public by offering up someone to blame other than the true culprit: the terrorists who had murdered Americans in cold blood.

When the final review closed, the only person with power who remained in Schwalier's corner was my boss.

During this same period, another incident was brewing, but this one was much closer to home and far less complicated than the Khobar Tower attack. But its results would be eerily the same.

A female B-52 pilot, Captain Kelly Flinn, at Minot Air Force Base in North Dakota, was accused of having an affair with an enlisted airman's spouse in her squadron. Although adultery is not uncommon or against the law in our society, the Department of Defense lists the offense as illegal for military members and punishable by a court-martial in accordance with the Uniformed Code of Military Justice.

Her commander, Lieutenant Colonel LaPlante, took all the appropriate actions in this matter, including a thorough investigation, which resulted in a number of charges against the pilot. In the commander's judgment, these charges warranted adjudication from a court-martial proceeding.

Similar to the aftermath of the Khobar Towers attack, the media began distorting the facts in order to create a political confrontation. The media spin was that the commander was being biased and inconsistent against a female officer for the antiquated charge of adultery. The controversy spiraled out of control, resulting in a Congressional hearing in which my boss correctly categorized this incident. On the record, he stated, "In the end, this is not an issue of adultery. This is an issue about an officer entrusted to fly nuclear weapons, that lied."[2]

Later, the secretary of the Air Force succumbed to the political pressure, took control of the situation, and offered the officer a general discharge from the Air Force, thereby stripping the commander of his duties under the Uniformed Code of Military Justice. The chief was publicly critical of the inappropriate actions taken by the secretary of the Air Force, his civilian supervisor, and fully supported the commander's actions in this situation.

These two events, occurring simultaneously under my boss's watch as the Air Force chief of staff, were defining moments for my understanding of courage as a leader.

As the senior uniformed Air Force officer, the chief was responsible for setting the example for the core values of the service: integrity first, service before self, and excellence in all we do. His actions taken during these two events epitomized the courage required of a leader who embodies these values.

After objectively reviewing all the facts in each matter, he was convinced that both commanders had acted with integrity, selflessly, and with excellence in serving their country, their units, and their fellow airmen. The chief knew the gravity of his situation and the ultimate consequences of his decisive actions to oppose both the unjust admonishment of Brigadier General Schwalier and the circumvention of Lieutenant Colonel LaPlante's command authority.

In the fall of 1997, the chief sent his letter of resignation to the secretary of the Air Force, almost a year prior to his scheduled tour of duty. After having served the nation honorably for over thirty-four years, he decided that keeping faith with his commanders was far more important than his allegiance to his supervisors. He put his legacy subservient to his responsibility to support the airmen he led. This is why he is still revered and respected as one of our most courageous chiefs among the ranks.

If, as Martin Luther King Jr. said, "The ultimate measure of a man is not where he stands in moments of comfort and convenience, but where he stands at times of challenge and controversy," then my boss is the ultimate measure of a man.

He stood firmly with his airmen.

TAKEAWAYS

- Courageous leaders seek the truth before acting.
- Courageous leaders are willing to sacrifice their legacy in order to do what's right.
- Courageous leaders stand up for and stand by their team.

CHAPTER 10

COURAGE IN THE LINE OF FIRE

H. D. "JAKE" POLUMBO

"Major Troy L. Gilbert distinguished himself by heroism while participating in aerial flight as an F-16CG pilot near Taji, Iraq on 27 November 2006. . . . He courageously supported U.S. Special Operations Forces by strafing insurgents in a hotly contested zone . . . and continued to press the insurgents with a second strafing pass which resulted in a fatal impact." —from the Distinguished Flying Cross citation with valor given posthumously to Major Troy L. Gilbert, who was killed in action during Operation Iraqi Freedom.

I DIDN'T PERSONALLY KNOW Troy "Trojan" Gilbert, but I know about his sacrifice. So do many of the Special Ops troops whose lives he saved during a firefight in Iraq. They still recount his story with great respect.

Four-star General Robin Rand, whom I've been friends with since 1979, told me the unabridged story of the courage

Troy displayed in the face of real and imminent danger on a fateful mission more than a decade ago. When Trojan met his untimely end, General Rand was Brigadier General Rand and commander of Troy's unit.

Prior to his deployment to Iraq in 2006, Major Gilbert was General Rand's executive officer at Luke Air Force Base near Phoenix, Arizona. Troy was also a flight instructor who loved flying F-16s and teaching young lieutenants how to pilot those incredible jets.

In the Air Force's storied fighter-pilot business, future leaders were often selected based on a combination of factors: notable flying skills, exceptional people skills, recent staff experience, continuous professional military education, and an in-depth understanding of the weapons and tactics involved in successful combat operations. But, ultimately, these leaders would not be successful as fighter squadron commanders if they couldn't actually *lead in battle*. General Rand exemplified these characteristics—and particularly the last principle.

He planned, led, and debriefed more missions than any other pilot in his earlier squadrons. He continued to teach and lead in the air at Luke AFB, even as the most senior pilot on the base. Consequently, Major Gilbert—like most of the pilots at Luke—greatly admired General Rand's leadership style. When General Rand was assigned as the 332nd Air Expeditionary wing commander at Joint Base Balad, just outside of Baghdad, for Operation Iraqi Freedom, Major Gilbert's loyalty to his boss compelled him to volunteer for the same deployment.

However, three issues should have precluded Troy's deployment.

First, Air Force instructor pilots in fighter training units usually weren't deployed to combat zones.

Preparing new fighter pilots was critical toward sustaining our war efforts in the Middle East. Generals at the Pentagon typically saw fit to leave our instructors stateside so the flow of new pilots to our war zones could continue uninterrupted. And it wasn't as if our instructors hadn't seen action: our experienced pilots had often recently returned from front-line duty at other bases—and those rotations, at that point in our military history, had usually included at least one combat tour in Iraq or Afghanistan. Troy was no exception.

Additionally, Major Gilbert was midway through his stateside assignment at Luke AFB. Most flight instructors would have served out their time stateside to keep the training squadron operations flowing smoothly.

Lastly—and I imagine this had to have been a difficult decision for Troy—he would deploy to Iraq while leaving his wife, Ginger, and his five children behind. But Troy felt compelled to follow his highly respected commander to Iraq to continue their mentor-protege relationship. The Air Staff in the Pentagon granted his request.

When Rand arrived at his new command in Iraq, he was quickly upgraded to flight lead and mission commander so that he could lead his troops in combat and demonstrate the courage and competence necessary to succeed in battle while handling the daily rigors of combat operations.

When Trojan arrived at Balad, he primarily concentrated on his flying responsibilities. The war in Iraq during that time was dynamic and relentless. Coalition soldiers on the ground faced constant danger. Our forces in the air had difficulty discerning friend from foe. But, by relying upon each other, we found success. The troops on the ground accomplished their difficult missions with the confidence that, within minutes of enemy contact, they could expect air support from Army or Marine attack helicopters or Air Force, Navy, or Marine jet fighters—including the F-16, which provided a large portion of air support across the war-torn country.

When Major Gilbert wasn't flying combat missions, he volunteered at the base's hospital, helping with resupply efforts and offering comfort to injured US and coalition troops. I have to imagine that seeing these catastrophic effects of the war seared images into Trojan's mind about just how dangerous the ground war was. Yet his resolve to serve his country never faltered.

That resolve would be put to the ultimate test on November 27, 2006.

Major Gilbert's Distinguished Flying Cross citation sets the stage for what would commence on Trojan's fateful run: "A crippled AH-6 helicopter and its crew were also in the area and in danger of being overrun." Troy's wingman had been on station, trying to support our ground troops, but he'd been unable to engage the enemy with his cannon. Consequently, as the most experienced member of the flight, Gilbert would have to use his advanced skills to roll in and precisely engage the enemy with 20-mm gunfire.

Every F-16 pilot can employ the cannon, but not every F-16 pilot has the skills to engage the enemy in danger-close combat the way Major Gilbert did that day, when their firefight had degraded into near chaos.

The citation continues: "Despite exposure to possible anti-aircraft fire, Major Gilbert immediately engaged the enemy with a strafing run against trucks." A strafing run in an F-16 is a dynamic, three-dimensional maneuver at speeds approaching

450 miles per hour—straight toward the ground. In addition to the possibility of being struck by enemy fire, the imminent danger of such high-speed, high-risk gun-runs is the threat of being unable to pull up in time.

After his first successful strafing pass, with his 20-mm gun cooling down from his recent burst, Major Gilbert recovered from his rapid descent just a few feet above the ground. As he pulled up to gain altitude and reset the attack, Major Gilbert kept an eye on the second of the three trucks employing heavy machine gun fire. Despite cockpit warnings regarding his proximity to the ground, he rolled in aggressively for a second, even tighter attack. Trojan again fired his cannon at the enemy—but this time he was unable to stop his descent before the aircraft struck the ground.

His courageous sacrifice clearly changed the course of the battle on the ground and his actions saved dozens of lives. The citation ends: "The outstanding heroism and selfless devotion to duty displayed by Major Gilbert in dedicated service to his country reflect great credit upon himself and the United States Air Force."

General Rand related to me that when he spoke to the US personnel who were on the ground, they told him, "When Troy arrived on scene, the whole situation changed for us." Later on, when he saw those same soldiers, they mentioned that, to this day, "Troy is revered in the special ops community... his picture hangs in the [Joint Special Operations Command] compound." This is a fitting tribute to an American airman who offered his life in defense of others. Many people state such an adage as one of their core values. Troy Gilbert lived it until he died.

Major Gilbert wasn't the only one who showed courage that day. The man he sought to emulate revealed a different form of courage in the aftermath of Troy's tragic death. According to unmanned aerial vehicle camera footage over the crash scene, enemy soldiers had quickly removed Major Gilbert's body from the site. But the USAF never leaves a man behind, and General Rand would not leave this hero behind.

In fact, General Rand assisted with the difficult responsibility of informing Troy's wife that he'd been shot down near Baghdad and was missing in action. He meticulously coordinated with the new commander at Luke Air Force Base—then Brigadier General Tom Jones—to make sure Ginger had every detail of the situation while the search and rescue team continued to look for her husband. And, even though it was not his responsibility, General Rand remained as the family liaison for ten more years, until Major Gilbert's remains were recovered, and he was given a proper military burial at Arlington National Cemetery on December 9, 2016.

According to General Mathew B. Ridgway, "There are two kinds of courage, physical and moral, and he who would be a true leader must have both. Both are the products of the character-forming process, of the development of self-control, self-discipline, physical endurance, of knowledge of one's job and, therefore, of confidence. These qualities minimize fear and maximize sound judgment under pressure—with some of that indispensable stuff called luck—often bringing success from seemingly hopeless situations."[1]

Major Troy "Trojan" Gilbert epitomized the physical courage required of all our military personnel when called to the duty of defending our nation. He had been taught this important leadership trait by skilled F-16 instructor pilots during countless training missions leading up to that fateful day in Iraq. He also showed a keen sense of leadership when he took control of the chaotic situation as his wingman was unable to deliver the firepower necessary to change the course of the battle on the ground.

General Robin Rand, his commander and mentor, demonstrated moral courage throughout his career when he repeatedly demonstrated the right way to lead, both in peacetime and in war.

Both of these individuals were courageous in their actions and are solid examples of leaders for their subordinates—and for all of us. We should be thankful we still have great Americans just like these two in our military today.

TAKEAWAYS

- Courageous leaders lead from the front, even in the heat of battle.
- Courageous leaders understand the risks *and* the rewards.
- Courageous leaders exhibit both physical and moral courage.

.

PART 3

COMPETENCE

CHAPTER 11

NOT THE SMARTEST PERSON IN THE ROOM

JAMES "REV" JONES

"I have always looked at my competencies before accepting any responsibility." —N. R. Narayana Murthy

---

WHEN I FIRST STARTED FLYING FIGHTERS, I read the biographies of the commanders I wanted to emulate. I soon realized they all had similar career paths.

For the first fifteen years of their respective careers, they established themselves as highly competent fighter pilots. Then they spent two to three years in non-flying staff assignments and attending professional military education before returning to the cockpit to command a squadron—the Air Force's basic war-fighting unit.

More often than not, the squadrons these leaders commanded were comprised of the aircraft they had flown earlier in their careers. To me, the path to a command position was clear: the most respected pilots were selected to lead our flying organizations.

At the time, it made perfect sense.

As it turns out, I couldn't have been more mistaken.

My early years in the Air Force followed that standard path.

I spent hours in the weapons vault studying the tactics, techniques, and procedures that would enable me to fully understand how best to employ my aircraft, as well as to know the strengths and weaknesses of potential adversary weapon systems so I could be effective in combat.

I sought out senior pilots and tacticians in the squadron who were willing to spend time with me so I could learn from their experiences.

I was selected to attend the Air Force Weapons School, an organization that takes the best operators from each weapons system and trains them, not only on how to employ their weapons systems at the highest skill levels but also, and most importantly, how to instruct others to reach the same levels of credibility. I subsequently spent three years as an instructor at the Weapons School itself. Ultimately, I was fortunate to become the commander of an operational F-16 squadron deployed to the Korean peninsula.

While in command, I never doubted (nor did the members of the squadron) that if we were called upon to execute our combat missions, I would lead the first flight on the first day against the toughest target, *and* I would have the most inexperienced pilot on my wing to help ensure he or she successfully accomplished the mission.

As such, I'm confident in saying I was a damned competent fighter pilot—but now I know that technical competence had very little to do with any modicum of success I may have had as a leader.

Leadership involves so much more than mere technical competence: motivating the people in your unit to do more than they thought possible, deriving a vision for the organization and inspiring others to willingly work toward attaining that vision, effective communication up and down the chain of command, the willingness to make tough decisions when required, driving change when it's required to remain relevant in a dynamic environment, and much more.

Those lessons were hard won though. I almost broke my neck to learn them.

Early in my career, the unexpected happened: I had to eject from my F-16.

I suffered neck damage that, after years of continued high G-force flying, would ultimately require surgery and the placement of metal retaining gear high on my neck. And that unfortunately occurred in the midst of my squadron command assignment.

Consequently, I was medically disqualified from flying ejection-seat aircraft. There would be no more fighter assignments for me.

I was devastated, both to lose the opportunity to do what I truly loved—flying fighter aircraft—and also because I was no longer on the perceived track to leadership I had tried to follow for years. I felt that, due to my disqualification, I wouldn't be able to command at higher levels and my career opportunities would be limited at best.

That's when I learned my earlier premise about pursuing senior leadership was all wrong.

Thankfully, the Air Force general officers with the responsibility to select the next generation of leaders knew they didn't need the best pilots to command a flying organization.

They needed flyers who knew how to lead.

As a result of their trust and confidence, I was honored to be given command over three wings, the Air Force's major warfighting organization. All three wings had different missions and were comprised of completely different types of aircraft.

My first wing was located in the Middle East and simultaneously supported air refueling and intelligence, surveillance, and reconnaissance (ISR) operations in Iraq and Afghanistan. The second wing provided air battle management using information derived from a ground-based, moving-target-indicator radar. The third wing was comprised of over seven thousand people geographically dispersed across the globe. It provided intelligence, surveillance, reconnaissance, electronic attack, and survivable command-and-control capabilities for national leadership and warfighters at all levels.

I was more than a little uncomfortable taking command of these organizations, as I knew the people within the wing had much more experience in the mission areas than I did. However, I knew my role wasn't to be the best tactician or crew member. My job was to lead.

As I took command of each organization, I first went through training in one of the aircraft types assigned to the wing and spent enough time doing so to enable me to safely fly with a basic level of competence. Though technical competence isn't the only aspect of leadership, I knew it was still an essential element in understanding the wing's mission and what would be required to attain mission success.

I've seen technical experts who were absolutely brilliant but would be challenged to lead four nuns in silent prayer. I am by no means denigrating the value these technical experts bring to the fight. They are often essential to the success of the organization. However, their value propositions did not necessarily require leadership roles within the organization.

I had no intention of becoming the best pilot in the wing. Even if I could have done so, that wasn't part of my job description anymore. After getting checked out in the aircraft, I focused on understanding the wing's mission and how we could best support the goals and objectives of the command echelons above the wing. I spent time in each of the subordinate units so I could understand how they contributed to the wing's mission and what their working conditions were like.

Most importantly, I looked for the formal and informal leaders within each unit—those who were committed to making their unit successful and who willingly accepted every challenge—and I empowered them.

In each case, I built a leadership team I could trust and depend on. I provided them with clearly defined goals and objectives, the metrics we'd use to measure success, and I did my best to provide the resources they needed to make success happen. I made sure they understood what decisions could and should be made at their level and what decisions and authorities needed to remain with me.

At that point, I put all of my effort toward helping them succeed. If they didn't have the right resources, the right people, or the right training, it was my responsibility to help them resolve the shortfalls. If they weren't able to meet stated goals and objectives because they didn't have what they needed, then I'd failed, not them. If they stumbled along the way, I did my best to help them up, dust them off, and get them back on track.

In all three cases, the wing was extraordinarily successful, largely because we were able to fully leverage the talent that resided within the organization.

I enjoyed being a line pilot more than you can imagine. However, there is no greater pleasure—or privilege—than helping an organization achieve its maximum potential.

That's what leaders do.

TAKEAWAYS

- Competent leaders do not have to be the technical expert nor the smartest person in the room.
- Competent leaders recognize their weaknesses and build a trusted, diverse leadership team to offset them.
- Competent leaders fully empower the formal and informal leaders within the organization and provide the resources required to enable their success.

CHAPTER 12

INFAMOUS FURNITURE

RICHARD "BEEF" HADDAD

"Man's flight through life is sustained by the power of his knowledge." —Austin "Dusty" Miller

---

IN THE FALL OF 2005, I received a call from my friend and mentor, Major General Frank Padilla. At the time, Frank was an Air Force Brigadier General tasked to start up the first post-Saddam Iraqi Air Force in Baghdad.

Prior to General Padilla's arrival, the "new" Iraqi Air Force —if you could call it that—had a small office in the Green Zone staffed by one Marine officer and one Army officer. The US had recently gifted three C-130s to establish their new air force and located them at Talil Air Base. Seventy or so American operators and maintenance personnel were training the Iraqis on the C-130s. But, surprisingly, no American airmen were overseeing the leadership of the new air force.

Not surprisingly, an aircraft accident happened at another base, starting the chain of events that led to my sudden departure for Baghdad. In the wake of the accident, Lieutenant General Walter E. Buchanan III, US Central Command Air Forces (CENTAF) commander, saw the need to include Air Force leadership in the standup of the new Iraqi Air Force. General Buchanan selected General Padilla to take on this task. Six months later, after conducting a strategy and planning review, General Padilla asked if I would supervise the build-up of the first C-130 air base.

I deployed and met General Padilla at Al Udeid Air Base in Qatar as he was rotating back to the states. For an hour, as General Padilla drew a chart on a napkin, we discussed the complex organizational structures I'd be contending with. He also relayed that the new air base would be at New Al Muthana, which was adjacent to the Baghdad airport and had been destroyed by US forces during the war. After our meeting, I realized my marching orders for the next six months had just been sketched on a napkin. Could something as complex as standing up a new Air Force Base in an unstable environment be simplified to a single, flimsy piece of paper?

I did have one ace up my sleeve: my Lebanese heritage. Many of the Iraqis viewed me as a cousin, and my Arabic was weak but passable. Once in Baghdad, I made fast friends quickly. I knew corruption was rampant, and I was cautious developing my trust in them, but my appearance, heritage, and friendly demeanor gave me the credibility I needed to embark on this immense job. In some areas, I'd be relying on their competence. In other areas, they'd have to rely on mine. If we were going to get it done in half a year, we needed to trust in and rely on each other.

The real work couldn't begin until our full coalition arrived in February. At that point, our team consisted of eleven Air Force airmen, an Army sergeant major, and a Danish supply sergeant. About thirty Iraqi airmen joined us, led by Brigadier General Karim Abood. We would develop a deep friendship over the course of this challenging project. The three C-130s from Talil arrived, along with 270 Iraqi and US airmen. Iraq's new air force was coming together in one place—or at least their planes were. But the air base itself was sorely lacking in resources even after the US had spent $40 million to upgrade the infrastructure.

I remember walking into that base, which was still something of a wreck, thinking how much we take for granted on already-established air bases: operations, maintenance, support, civil engineering, security—the list goes one. None of that was yet in place. At New Al Muthana, all we had were willing men and women who wanted to see that air base transformed. Even though the initial investment by our government got us necessities, that base was really built on the cornerstones of competence, trust, and relationships.

For instance, I observed the base had a majority of Sunni Muslims and asked General Karim why. He told me the Iraqi Air Force did not hire based on religious preference but rather on competence for the task. Because Saddam Hussein was a Sunni, many of the most experienced airmen were Sunni. In light of Iraq's recent past, I expected to see more Shiites. In fact, General Karim was Shiite. But he reminded me, "We need to select based on skill level."

The competence of the Iraqis of both religious factions shone through, a fact for which I was grateful then and remain grateful today. Together, they joined the effort to build the base so they could show they served their country, not their former dictator. They were dedicated to their mission and the new

Iraqi constitution. They were all proud of who they were and what they were accomplishing.

I leaned heavily on building, growing, and maintaining strong working relationships with all these people, and it made me think back to the words inscribed on the Eagle and Fledgling statue at the Air Force Academy—except my version is: "Man's flight through life is sustained by the power of his *relationships*." This isn't to dismiss the importance of knowledge; it's to underscore that knowledge without effective working relationships is often useless. This is especially true in a foreign country attempting a daunting task with an internationally diverse group of people.

We coupled the wide range of knowledge we had with relationships that created a burning desire to excel. In six months, we had all the support organizations a new Air Force Base needed in place.

In fact, I believe we did such a good job that we established a new standard for scheduling, setting benchmarks, and aligning tasks for future Air Force Bases that needed to be erected. My backing for that claim? In the fall of 2005, General Padilla asked me to tackle the same task, but in Afghanistan. This time, I was on the initial team that brainstormed the best strategy-to-task methodology for the future of the Afghan Army Air Corps. It was amazing to be part of that effort, just as it was in Iraq, and to see the same professionalism and competence in action in Afghanistan.

One indelible memory stands out from both experiences.

While working on the base at New Al Muthana, I'd made sure to develop relationships with everyone I could, including the State Department personnel. While visiting their annex one day, I saw they were getting rid of a lot of furniture that seemed to be in good shape. One of the State Department folks told me they were switching it out for more Western office furniture and were throwing the "old" furniture away. As early as Operation Desert Storm, I'd learned to look for opportunities to scrounge and barter for what we needed, from tents to cots to lumber for sidewalks.

The State Department employee must have seen my face light up, because he immediately asked, "You want it?"

"Absolutely!"

After borrowing a big truck and a couple of airmen from Sather Air Base, the large US base adjacent to New Al Muthana, we loaded the truck with our newfound treasure. When we drove up, dozens of Iraqis crowded around, talking excitedly and looking amazed. I thought, *Are they really this excited about furniture?* We spent the next few hours offloading the furniture and spreading it around our sparsely furnished base offices.

That night, General Karim asked me, "Do you know why the men were so happy to see this furniture?"

I replied, "Because we had nowhere to sit?"

"They know this was Saddam's furniture," General Karim said.

I was silent. I hadn't known.

General Karim smiled. "You know, Colonel Haddad, your success in achieving all this is due to the relationships you've developed, and we are extremely thankful."

I sat back in my new chair and contemplated how far we'd all come—together.

TAKEAWAYS

- Competent leaders trust the proven competence of their teams.
- Competent leaders leverage their competencies to establish points of connection.
- Competent leaders form effective working relationships.

CHAPTER 13

THE CREDIBILITY OF PROFICIENCY

TOM "HONEZ" JONES

"Flying by instruments soon outgrew the early experimental phase. I was grateful for the opportunity to participate in the initial experiments. This work was, I believe, my most significant contribution to aviation." —Jimmy Doolittle

---

WHEN OPERATION IRAQI Freedom began in March of 2003, I was the wing commander at Al Jaber Air Base in Kuwait. For months before the conflict, we had furiously prepared for the possibility of war. One issue loomed large.

With almost two hundred aircraft on base, our weapons storage area had become overwhelmed. We expanded the area and worked to protect it from attacks, but we were physically unable to meet the exacting weapons safety standards mandated by regulations.

About a month before the war began, a safety officer inspected our site. In so many words, I was told, "You're in violation of multiple portions of the safety regulations. I'll have to report this to your commander, as well as the Air Staff." In other words, he'd be telling my boss, Lieutenant General Moseley, and the Pentagon that our base presented multiple risks due to our inability to store our overflowing weapons safely.

However, I knew that my team had done everything within our power to mitigate the risks associated with these violations. Preempting the safety report, I got word to General Moseley expressing my views. He replied with his full confidence in my abilities and that he was fine with whatever I decided needed to be done about the situation.

With that reassurance, we continued to prepare for combat. Ultimately, the issue became a nonissue. Even if the Pentagon had expressed concern, I am certain that General Moseley would have backed me up. He trusted my competence and thus my ability to lead, a faith that I remain grateful for.

As combat became a certainty, I came to appreciate General Moseley's trust even more. He granted me, as well as all of his other wing commanders, the authority to deviate from certain restrictions imposed upon pilots during peacetime operations. For instance, if I thought it necessary, I could extend our pilots' duty day beyond twelve hours. I could waive the penalty (grounding) for overdue check rides (demonstrating competency in the mission set) until after combat was completed. And I could allow maintenance professionals to postpone mandatory inspections until combat was completed.

I was grateful for his trust because it allowed me—and the squadrons operating under my control—the flexibility to execute wartime tasking. By its nature, combat requires taking more risks that we don't accept during peacetime or noncombat operations. Had the restrictions not been lifted, I would have been unable to meet the heightened demands that combat imposes.

During my time serving General Moseley, I never questioned why he allowed me such leeway when it came to those restrictions. But, after having spoken with the man numerous times after the conclusion of Operation Iraqi Freedom, I learned that he granted my requests because he had faith in the competence of his subordinate leaders. In fact, he'd handpicked each one of us, knowing that our respective records of service and leadership would lead us to do the right thing at the right time. As we faced challenging situations in combat, the competence we'd displayed earlier in our careers had served as his foundation for the latitude he granted us to lead as we saw fit.

When I consider General Moseley's leadership, I likewise see his competence. He had distinguished himself at all levels, tactically and professionally. He was a graduate of the Air Force's toughest flying course, the Fighter Weapons Instructor Course, then later returned to command the F-15 Division, a command challenge reserved for our most talented flyers and leaders. He performed so well that he was selected seven years later to command the entire wing—another of our most challenging commands. His successes led to demanding assignments on the Joint Staff and Air Staff, where he continued to excel.

Today's Air Force was borne of such leaders like him, men and women who achieved tactical greatness and transferred it to organizational success. Three historical examples, all from the early twentieth century, spring to mind.

The tactical proficiency that Billy Mitchell, Jimmy Doolittle, and Claire Chennault all showed gave them the credibility to make major changes in how airpower was wielded as a national instrument of power. Without their high competence in flying, coupled with their determination to lead despite opposition, I'm convinced the Air Force would not be what it is today.

Lionized as one of the pioneers of airpower, Billy Mitchell witnessed Orville Wright fly at Fort Myer, Virginia, in 1908, when Mitchell was just a young officer in the Army's Signal Corps. He became instantly enamored by the possibilities of flight. Eight years later, and with the Army considering him too old by then to enter flight training, Mitchell acquired a pilot's license at his own expense.[1]

When America entered World War I in 1918, Mitchell was the first American officer to fly over German lines. In September of 1918, he planned and led a coordinated attack in support of the Saint-Mihiel offensive by fifteen hundred US, British, Italian, and French aircraft. By the end of the war, he was promoted to brigadier general and commanded all American air combat units in France.[2]

No one could deny Mitchell's tactical prowess and stellar combat achievements. He consequently set about using his competence to advocate, fearlessly and vocally, for his controversial theories (at the time) of airpower and its application in warfare. He believed that airpower should belong alongside land and sea power for national defense. He proved himself when he showed how vulnerable the US Navy could be by orchestrating an airpower test that led to the sinking of the SMS *Ostfriesland*, a captured German WWI battleship, in July of 1921.[3] The feat astonished both political and military leadership.[4] However, his unrelenting and outspoken advocacy for airpower eventually resulted in his court-martial and subsequent resignation from the Army.[5]

But public and professional opinions supported Mitchell's beliefs. His arguments continued to be advanced, and they were ultimately adopted, even though Mitchell was out of uniform by then. In fact, as a late admission to the value of his opinions, Mitchell was posthumously promoted to major general and awarded a Medal of Honor.[6] His tactical competence and acceptance by both the public and his colleagues (though not his superiors) enabled Mitchell to make monumental and long-lasting changes to airpower and its use in war.

In a similar vein, and in a similar timeframe, Jimmy Doolittle also leveraged his reputation to advance airpower. In 1918, Doolittle entered the military and learned to fly. He quickly became an instructor pilot and was one of the best-known pilots during the years between the end of WWI and the beginning of WWII. He'd even achieved national acclaim for his coast-to-coast flights and high-speed races.[7]

Doolittle may be best known and revered as the man who led the 1942 raid on Japan,[8] but I could argue that his greatest contribution to aviation was his study, design, and integration of instrumentation that allows pilots—even today—to fly in bad weather conditions. Doolittle was a visionary who understood that flight, to reach its fullest potential, could not be limited only to flying in good weather.

To that end, and armed with his masters and doctorate in aeronautics, as well as public support, Doolittle researched how pilots became disoriented in inclement weather. He then helped to develop instruments that indicate an artificial horizon —instrumentation that's still used today. Putting his competence to its truest test in 1929, Doolittle became the first pilot to take off, fly, and land his aircraft based solely on the use of his instrumentation.[9]

Doolittle actually solved two problems with his invention: how to fly in bad weather and how to bridge the untrusting gap between the engineers who built the airplanes and the pilots who flew them (a problem that's likely persisted since the beginning of manned flight). Doolittle wrote, "In the early '20s, there was not complete support between the flyers and the engineers. The pilots thought the engineers were a group of people who zipped slide rules back and forth, came out with erroneous results and bad aircraft; and the engineers thought the pilots were crazy—otherwise they wouldn't be pilots."[10] Doolittle bridged that great divide due to his reputation and acceptance as a tactical genius. Because he was an intelligent engineer as well as an accomplished pilot, his words and his work transcended functional barriers and brought airpower to greater military and commercial relevance.

Lastly, consider General Claire Chennault, who earned his wings in 1919 and eventually became an accomplished pursuit pilot. (Pursuit pilots are what we now call fighter pilots.) In the 1930s, as Chief of Pursuit Section at the Air Corps Tactical School, he led a nationally acclaimed exhibition flying team. That's where he also theorized and wrote that pursuit aircraft could defeat bomber formations, a notion that ran counter to airpower beliefs of his day.

He resigned from the Army in 1937 due to poor health (chiefly deafness due to flying) and, ostensibly, having been passed over for promotion to Major. However, he was quickly recruited by the Chinese to go to China and train their aviators. He soon became the chief air advisor to Chiang Kai-shek, the president of the Republic of China. In 1941, his relationship with the Chinese led to his appointment as the commander of the American Volunteer Group, a.k.a the Flying Tigers.

Knowing that his physical limitations prevented him from

flying with his outfit during combat, Chennault focused on intense training during peacetime so that his airmen would perform well in combat. He was reported to have been a demanding taskmaster, but his tactical reputation enabled him to impart his beliefs about fighting as a team in their P-40 aircraft. Other air forces tended to train and fight as individuals, thus leaving themselves vulnerable to coordinated attacks from two different aircraft. Chennault believed that two aircraft operating as a closely-knit team could succeed in engagements with adversaries who possessed greater numbers and even more technically advanced aircraft.

Putting those beliefs to the test, Chennault's squadron succeeded by any definition of winning aerial combat, especially when fighting against Japanese pilots who were arguably flying better aircraft. Ultimately, Chennault's well-earned laurels as a tactician and pilot allowed him to train and lead an organization that affected the strategic outcomes in the Pacific Theater of WWII.

Of Mitchell, Doolittle, and Chennault, only Doolittle enjoyed the support and respect of his superior officers. Mitchell and Chennault had such rocky relationships with their superiors that it ultimately led to their early exits from uniformed service.

I was fortunate to have superiors more like Doolittle's, whose faith in my competence was both reassuring and rewarding. In time, as I became a higher-ranking leader, General Moseley's trusting leadership was my model.

I can only hope that the commanders below me benefitted from my trust in their competence as much as I benefitted from General Moseley's trust in me.

· · ·

TAKEAWAYS

- Competent leaders place confidence in their proven subordinates.
- Competent leaders excel at their talents and never stop pursuing excellence.
- Competent leaders motivate similar competence in future leaders.

CHAPTER 14

WHAT'S IN YOUR SOCK?

ROB "MUMBLES" POLUMBO

"Competence goes beyond words. It's the leader's ability to say it, plan it, and do it in such a way that others know that you know how—and know that they want to follow you." — John C. Maxwell

---

IN 1986, I arrived at Kunsan Air Base in the Republic of Korea for my first fighter assignment. I was a qualified—but still green—F-16 pilot and brand-new second lieutenant. I had been assigned to the 8th Tactical Fighter Wing, "The Wolf Pack," recognized as one of the most competent combat units established after World War II.

After meeting my first operational wing commander, Colonel Nels Running, "The Wolf," it was immediately evident that he viewed the mission of the Air Force—to fly, fight, and win—as his highest priority. He also knew it was the commander's responsibility to set the tone for the entire unit.

The Wolf, through his diligent desire to lead through competence, *always* led the pack from the front.

The Wolf flew. The Wolf fought. The Wolf won.

This was made apparent to me on a day I'll never forget.

On one of my first flights to be tested as a mission-ready combat pilot, I was paired with two other aviators—and The Wolf. In fact, his name was on the scheduling board as the lead position of our four-ship sortie the next day. The day prior to our flight, he sent another airman to ask me why I wasn't with him in the map room preparing for the mission.

I double-timed to the squadron-planning room. The commander was preparing low-level maps, developing our ingress/egress plan, and determining the best weapons-and-attack profile to destroy our planned target for the mission. As soon as he saw me, he wasted no time in explaining his tactical plans in minute detail, providing me with specific reasons for his every decision. I quickly ascertained that each of his tactics was based on the objective of providing our flight with the highest probability to kill and survive the threat scenario.

I thought, *I want to follow this Wolf.*

With The Wolf leading our charge the next day, we executed the flight flawlessly. His superior mission preparation, down to the smallest detail, had ensured our success. But his unrivaled leadership didn't end there.

After landing, The Wolf called us into the squadron debriefing room and discussed each aspect of the mission with us. Every detail was dissected to determine if we had fulfilled our directed responsibilities. For any breakdown in flight discipline or noncompliance with the plan, The Wolf sternly asked the airman at fault for an explanation. Then The Wolf reviewed every airman's videotape to ensure all weapons employment had met the rules of engagement and was valid for killing the intended target. Finally, the debrief culminated in a list of lessons learned and an overall assessment of our main objective: Did we kill and survive?

That day, with that commander, may have been the most impactful event of my career in the Air Force. The Wolf's expert competency, articulate explanations of his planning, in-flight leadership, and insightful debriefing were character qualities I wanted to emulate. I was also impressed that such a combat-proven colonel, with many other responsibilities, would take the time to pass on his vast experience and knowledge to a fledgling lieutenant.

But The Wolf understood the magnitude of his position.

In just one month, I'd been qualified as a combat-mission-ready F-16 pilot capable of employing all the weapons in the inventory—including a nuclear bomb. In other words, at the ripe old age of twenty-three, I was given the responsibility to deliver a weapon with the explosive firepower that was seventeen times as powerful as the atomic bomb that had been dropped on Nagasaki.

As much as this new responsibility weighed on my shoulders, I can't imagine how it must have felt to The Wolf. He wasn't just responsible for teaching me well; he was responsible for our entire Wolf Pack. Consequently, The Wolf insisted that every member of the team, no matter the job one had in the wing, lead with his same vigor and level of competence.

Unsurprisingly, The Wolf's competencies that I saw and experienced in the air extended to his leading of an air base in a foreign country only a couple of hundred miles away from the enemy. His desire to be the most competent airman he could be positively influenced everyone else in the unit likewise to be their best. It came as no surprise that The Wolf culminated his exemplary career as a two-star general.

But, in considering this man's legacy, the career paths of his subordinates might be even more compelling.

Of the seventy airmen I knew during my one-year assignment with the Wolf Pack, fourteen went on to graduate from the prestigious Weapons Instructor Course. Only 1 percent of *all* pilots in the Air Force are even selected for this course. Ten airmen became general officers, including The Wolf's deputy from that time, who became a four-star commander of Pacific Air Forces.

And, I am convinced that my rise to major general emanated from my early lessons from The Wolf. To this day, I will argue that our Wolf Pack was one of the most combat-capable units the Air Force ever produced—not because of the men in the group, but because of the man who led the group.

I was spoiled for future wing commanders by having served under The Wolf so early in my tenure with the Air Force. Over the remainder of my career, only a few commanders measured up to the high bar The Wolf had set. However, the ones who did measure up—the ones who put forth the effort to lead from the front and continued to develop their competencies over their careers—were the ones who'd ultimately become general officers and leaders of our Air Force.

Because of my memorable experiences as part of the Wolf Pack, when I think of leadership, I first think of competence. To me, there's no other characteristic more important to the suitability of a person to lead than their grasp of the task at hand. I

can't think of a more compelling attribute than supreme competence that exudes the mantra of "Come, follow me!"

Reflecting upon the many people placed in leadership roles
throughout my career, I can't think of one in my top-five list
who didn't exhibit complete competence in all facets of their
daily performance. For me, competence is the basic foundation
of every notable leader. In fact, the depth and breadth of an
individual's understanding of an entire scheme are what I first
notice when evaluating a person's propensity to lead.

Developing competence in one's craft takes daily initiative,
discipline, and work ethic. The people who exhibit these characteristics set themselves apart from their peers and are easily
noticed as future leaders. In the fighter-pilot world, these individuals are the first to be upgraded to flight leader. As their
competence expands and encompasses more and more of the
flight-operations business, they're selected for the higher supervisory roles of instructors, mission commanders, and flight-eval-
uation pilots. By necessity, each level requires more in-depth
experience, knowledge, and understanding.

I describe this constant vigilance and thirst for more knowledge, experience, and skills as "filling your sock." Every day,
those who seek competence should take whatever new information, experiences, and lessons they've learned and place them
into *their* sock. One should also include the rich experiences of
their mentors, coaches, and those with whom they work, who
can all provide exponential increases in the contents of their
sock. After a while, it's easy to recognize individuals who've
made concerted efforts to fill their socks. Ultimately, they
always overshadow their peers.

My sock is still filled with the observations and mentoring I received from The Wolf way back in Korea. His words, teachings, and example prepared me for my future leadership positions, both within the Air Force and in my civilian life. I learned then that developing competence is not a spurious, one-time endeavor but rather a never-ending, lifelong pursuit.

Competence is an essential requirement of leadership, so never stop filling your sock!

TAKEAWAYS

- Competent leaders challenge their followers to pursue greater skill at their job.
- Competent leaders demand of themselves exactly what they expect from their team.
- Competent leaders never stop learning.

CHAPTER 15

COWBOY COMPETENCE

H. D. "JAKE" POLUMBO

"Whenever you are asked if you can do a job, tell 'em, 'Certainly I can!' Then get busy and find out how to do it." —Theodore Roosevelt

---

RETIRED MAJOR GENERAL BOB "COWBOY" DuLaney epitomizes competence in leadership. A proud leader with a distinctive style, he demanded a high level of performance and skill from himself first, then his subordinates second. I know this because, when he was a lieutenant colonel and colonel, I was his subordinate for many years over the course of multiple assignments during my thirty-four-year career in the U.S. Air Force.

In 1990, I was chosen to return to the prestigious USAF Fighter Weapons School at Nellis Air Force Base in Nevada to become an instructor pilot. I was a graduate of that same program, after having mastered the F-16's many missions, from delivering tactical nuclear weapons to providing offensive counter-air alongside other aircraft, to ensuring the US could defend bases with defensive combat air patrol missions.

The Fighter Weapons School was the premiere instructor training course. When Air Combat Command formed in 1992, the school changed its focus on fighter aviation, dropped *Fighter* from its title, and became the Air Force Weapons School. The name change occurred because courses had been designed and implemented for many other war-fighting skills besides what I loved best: flying fighter aircraft. The Air Force had to increase the size of the school, not only to train new instructors in fighter aircraft but also to train new instructors of bomber crews and other types of weapons systems. Today, the Weapons School has twenty-one squadrons operating from nine different locations around the US, with only a third of their students coming from the service's fighter bases.

After I graduated from the Weapons School in 1987, I was assigned to the 36th Fighter Squadron at Osan Air Base in South Korea. Our squadron was named "The Fabulous Flying Fiends," the "Fiends" for short, and I was truly honored to be in the same squadron my father had flown in during his hundred combat missions in the Korean War.

During my first of two assignments on the Korean peninsula, I was selected to go back to Weapons School as an instructor. It was an honor I gladly accepted, but, to be honest, I was a little intimidated by the prospect of teaching at such a prestigious school.

That's where I met Cowboy DuLaney.

When I arrived, the F-16 division was in full transition from one commander to another, from a limited set of learning objectives to a full, multi-role syllabus that would make the six-month course the most demanding in the school. Our new commander was a matter-of-fact fighter pilot with an impressive record in both the F-16, a.k.a. the Viper, and the F-4, a.k.a. the Phantom.

Now, you may be wondering: Why do our planes have nicknames?

In the late 70s, when the F-16 first came into the Air Force inventory, the air staff at the Pentagon went through its official naming process for its newest fighter and ultimately designated the aircraft as the Fighting Falcon. But, as is often the case in the military, users and admirers of the new fighter overruled this Pentagon decision and began calling the jet the Viper due to its sleek look. And its stunning frontal profile reminded people of a snake on the attack. Plus, the ease with which the alternative name flowed out of peoples' mouths helped the new nickname catch on.

As someone who flew a Viper for decades, the name was fitting. Over the course of my career, I flew the Viper from one hundred feet above the ground to fifty thousand feet, and even all the way up to Mach 2.0 on one of my final training missions over the Atlantic Ocean in 2015.

When I learned that Cowboy was to be my division commander at Weapons School, I was thrilled. He was already known across the fighter world then, and he was respected by all of the other fighter commands, from the proven F-4 community full of Vietnam War vets to the F-15 Eagle community who truly believed they were flying the world's finest fighter. There was always a heated rivalry between the Viper drivers and the Eagle pilots in the Nellis bar on Friday nights.

I would quickly learn why Cowboy DuLaney was so well-regarded.

Lieutenant Colonel DuLaney was a gifted fighter pilot, and he flew often to hone his impressive skills. But if he made a mistake in the air during one of his training missions, he immediately fessed up to it in the debrief and offered some thoughts as to how he would avoid the same mistake on the next mission. He was continually trying to improve his own flying skills. It was a refreshing technique compared to those employed by other, more seasoned pilots, who rarely admitted their own mistakes and whose skills were diminishing daily as they sat in their office and did paperwork.

Now, if Cowboy observed mistakes by his other instructors during workups for the classes, he'd give that pilot a chance to admit his own mistake in the debrief. But, if it wasn't forthcoming, Cowboy would correct them on the spot, in front of all the others in the room—including other instructors.

As we taught the new group of F-16 instructors how to hone their skills and make the entire combat Air Force better, Cowboy's example became one of our most distinctive calling cards: First, train hard and push yourself to the limit. Next, admit your own mistakes. Only then have you earned the right to call out mistakes by others.

This single factor, championed by our boss, significantly raised the level of performance in the rest of the division and gave us the street credibility so important in such a schoolhouse. Once younger fighter pilots realized that Cowboy was going to own up to his mistakes, they knew they had to do the same thing, and that calculus made everyone better. When the boss's competence and integrity are at the highest levels, the rest of the organization will raise its collective performance to previously unattainable levels.

We had to admit our mistakes because Cowboy did not allow for excuses or obfuscation. He continually reminded us that coming in second in our business was losing. He told us that the nation expected us to win 99–1, not 51–49. Our victories had to be decisive, which meant our mistakes had to be eradicated. Flying a Viper required nothing less.

Again, Cowboy modeled this for us. His most impressive skill may have been that he continually led the toughest training sessions and was always on point as we tried to refine our syllabus and scenarios to extract the most out of each and every flight.

During one critical phase of training called Air-to-Air Combat Maneuvering and Tactics Training, Cowboy took painstaking effort at getting the F-16 pilots to learn how to use a new long-range air-to-air missile. Previously, the F-16 Viper only carried short-range heat-seeking missiles available for air-to-air combat. When the long-range AIM-120 Advanced Medium-Range Air-to-Air Missile (AMRAAM) came into the F-16 inventory, Cowboy ensured our techniques for using the missile would be both lethal against the enemy and accepted by field commanders. These general officers were the ones who would set the rules of engagement that would allow F-16 pilots to shoot real AMRAAMs at the enemy, even if friendlies were in the area.

As we refined our employment standards and training scenarios, Cowboy would inevitably lead the next mission to fully validate our new tactics. If we discovered a problem in the outcome of a particular mission, Cowboy would spend countless hours working out the fixes to ensure we had it right. He was a patient leader at times, especially when others were confident enough to suggest new ideas about how to better use the missile. He knew he didn't have all the right answers, and so other ideas were always welcome in a debrief led by Cowboy.

In the end, we refined our tactics and procedures and ultimately published the book[1] on how to use the AMRAAM in combat for the multi-role F-16. These tactics would prove critical in the next decade of continuous combat operations in the Middle East for the United States Air Force.

Lastly, I also learned a great deal from Cowboy's leadership skills during a time when all-altitude day-and-night flying operations were still expected from every Viper pilot. His skills and competence at low altitude were recognized across the combat air forces.

On any given training mission up on the Nevada Tactics and Training Ranges, many Viper pilots learned that the true low-altitude operating level was not three hundred to five hundred feet above the ground, where they normally flew at speeds of five hundred miles an hour; the low block was actually *one hundred to two hundred* feet above the ground at treetop level, where the enemy was unlikely to see you until it was too late. This was Cowboy's block of airspace, and we all knew we had to prove our own competence in this high-risk area of operation.

Lieutenant Colonel DuLaney was simply the best in the division at employing from low altitude, and we all knew it. He was the best fighter pilot in the division during those years, and that high degree of competence in his profession made him our unchallenged leader.

Competent leaders need to be good at what they do, really good—just as Cowboy out-piloted us all in the Air Force's premier training program. Such leaders need a high degree of certainty and confidence in both their actions and the guidance they give as they proceed through their tenure as the boss.

Competent leaders also need to be willing to show their subordinates how to do things, not merely tell them how good they used to be. Leaders should arrange their daily and weekly schedules to ensure they have adequate time to talk things over with the staff and ultimately walk them through the best way to operate, whether it's designing and building products or employing a high-performance fighter at low altitude and extremely high speeds with the newest and finest missile on their wing.

Additionally, when new equipment or techniques come into the equation, competent leaders need to be on point, out front, making critical decisions on how the team should use the new technology. And good leaders should never feel intimidated by new people in the organization offering innovative ideas and suggestions. Rather, leaders should embrace these highly skilled people who merely want to become an integral part of high-performance teams.

I know for a fact I would not have been such a capable instructor and future leader were it not for the competent, unrivaled example of Bob DuLaney.

Thanks, Cowboy!

TAKEAWAYS

- Competent leaders readily admit their mistakes so others can learn from them.
- Competent leaders lead by setting the bar high and always enforcing standards.
- Competent leaders don't live in the past; they show subordinates the way forward by their own example.

PART 4

COMPASSION

CHAPTER 16

CARING FOR THE ENEMY

H. D. "JAKE" POLUMBO

"Be kind, for everyone you meet is fighting a harder battle." —Plato

---

NEARLY EVERY TIME I visited Bagram Air Base, the base commander, then Brigadier General Joseph T. "Gus" Guastella, met me at the helicopter landing pad at the southwest end of the runway. We'd salute, shake hands, and then get to work. It was always nice to see Gus. We'd known each other from our previous deployments to the Middle East and from various flying exercises around the US. Plus, I much more preferred catching up on important matters face-to-face rather than through the secure video-conferencing device we used most every other day.

On one memorable visit in April 2013 to the 455th Air Expeditionary Wing, the commander leaned over to me as we rode to his office located at the center of the base. He said, "One of our HH-60s just brought in three severely wounded troops. IED attack earlier today. Think you could go visit them?"

I nodded my head. "Of course."

As commander of the 9th Air and Space Expeditionary Task Force–Afghanistan, I supervised nearly five thousand airmen and five organizations. This included the largest US military base in Afghanistan: Bagram Air Base, just six miles southeast of Charikar. The base's single runway at the time could handle any of our US aircraft, from Lockheed Martin C5 Galaxies to Sikorsky HH-60 Pave Hawk helicopters. During my deployment, the base was home to tens of thousands of US and NATO troops. Since so many key operations emanated from the airfield, I visited the base one or two times a week. My job was to manage and lead these airmen, but I knew that my position required boosting morale too.

So, of course I would take the time to speak with our wounded soldiers.

After getting my OK, Gus drove us to the base's hospital. Sporting fifty beds, the Heathe N. Craig Joint Theater Hospital was named after a US Army medic, Staff Sergeant Heathe N. Craig, who gave up his life while trying to save a fellow soldier in combat operations near Bagram. The hospital, which is still in use today, features modern facilities that our soldiers would expect to find at home.

Once we arrived, the hospital commander and chief nurse greeted us. Before they'd even spoken a word, I considered what truly impressive Americans they were, using their skills and talent to serve in a place like this. I was genuinely pleased to meet them—even under the circumstances that were tearing that country apart and wreaking havoc on our soldiers.

After we exchanged greetings, the hospital commander said, "General Polumbo, the prognoses for the soldiers who just arrived is guarded. In fact, one of the injured just had his left leg amputated."

Even though this was part of the job, and I'd heard and seen a number of seriously injured soldiers, I was still nervous about the upcoming encounter.

The commander continued. "He's in a great deal of pain. He's on a morphine drip, and I think he's still disoriented from the attack and the rescue op."

I nodded my head. All three soldiers were in the same room together, but only the one with the missing leg was really awake. The others were asleep or sedated too much to talk with.

I walked into the room, still unsure of what I would say but knowing that any encouragement from me could help this young man who had given so much for his country.

As I stood in front of the awake young man, I could tell he was in a lot of pain and truly in distress. He stared at his missing leg in disbelief. I told him that he had the best doctors and nurses available anywhere and that he was going to get better. I also said, "We'll get you in touch with your family as soon as possible and tell them we're doing everything in our power to take care of their son and his buddies, and we'll get the three of you back safely to the US."

The soldier nodded his head and whispered his thanks.

I squeezed his hand a little, and then he closed his eyes and drifted off again.

I think my words made a difference, but it's always hard to tell. Within twenty-four hours, he was on a military C-17 headed to a hospital in Germany. I guessed that he'd be back in the states within a couple of days.

When I returned to speak with the hospital commander

and chief nurse, I learned something troubling but not unexpected for Craig hospital: a wounded Taliban soldier was in the same ward.

To make matters more confusing, a wounded female Afghan civilian was also in the hospital, along with her unharmed young son. I guessed they were there due to the same IED attack that had injured our soldiers—which might have even been placed by the Taliban soldier recovering in a heavily guarded room just down the hall. And the hospital's professionals were caring for him just like they would have had he been a US Army soldier.

Talk about surreal.

Then again, considering Bagram's central location in that war-torn country, it was probably just another normal day for that outstanding staff. But what an illustration for the necessity of genuine compassion by our medical leaders.

The care and concern of these two officers was truly remarkable, as was the care from the rest of the staff who were helping the victims of the same attack. These were brave, competent US service members who did their job in rugged and demanding conditions, and they never seemed to outwardly struggle with the irony of the situation.

After the brief meeting with the wounded soldiers, I gathered the staff in the entryway of the hospital. "Hello, airmen!" I continued, "I hope you know how much I appreciate what you're doing here. It's an incredible situation that I've just witnessed—all these different people from the one battle being cared for inside the same hospital ward."

I paused to scan the crowd and make eye contact one by one, as best I could, and continued. "I appreciate the compassion you're showing these people. You make me proud, and you make the citizens back home very proud."

Then I turned to the commander and the chief nurse. "Thanks for your selfless service and impressive leadership. You set a high bar for your staff to reach for and demonstrate what it means to be US service members overseas in a combat zone."

I glanced down before looking back at the group and then mentioned how proud their family members would be, especially if they knew how each of them were handling their duties in the difficult conditions I'd just observed. "Other Americans, once they hear this story, will be impressed with your dedication and service."

I always tried to keep these "all-calls" relaxed and informal when possible. Sometimes, I'd pass out my commander's coin to a deserving airman if the situation warranted. I often used my engraved coin as a memento for the best airmen in a unit, a time-honored tradition in the military that still happens today all over the world. But this was an impromptu visit, and I imagine just hearing words of praise from me instead of the patients' painful needs was a welcome departure from their norm.

I finished with a quick update on the current operations the International Security Assistance Force (ISAF) had underway. I warned the airmen that "nothing's gonna get any easier in the weeks and months to come. Likely, it'll stay very difficult." I finished by reminding them how important their jobs were to the overall success of ISAF's mission.

They nodded in determined silence. These men and women understood what they were signing up for and were prepared to make the sacrifice.

"Do you have any questions for me?"

A few hands went up.

I fielded typical questions about what was happening in Kabul, the capital of Afghanistan, and what was going on at the ISAF headquarters, where I worked on a daily basis. I did the best I could to explain how we were operating, why we had chosen that course of action, and what we were doing in the planning sessions and staff meetings that went on day and night at the headquarters.

Each of the men and women standing in front of me accepted my summary in due course. None seemed to grumble or in any way complain about their conditions.

Again, I was impressed by their poise and attitude. The staff of Craig Joint Hospital operated in a way that professionally exemplified what US men and women regularly do in combat operations.

After all their questions had been answered, the commander escorted General Guastella and me out of the hospital and thanked us for the visit.

I should have been the one thanking him, and so I did just that. I felt good about the opportunity Gus had arranged to see those compassionate officers in action—to watch their leadership and to see how important it was for them to take care of their staff, the dedicated men and women who were accomplishing the mission every day.

That commander and chief nurse exemplified such a critical component of strong leadership to me: genuine compassion for people in need. They cared for *any human being* injured in combat operations, anybody in a dire situation—even if it was an enemy Taliban soldier.

.   .   .

TAKEAWAYS

- Compassionate leaders make time to show real concern for other people.
- Compassionate leaders don't fear wearing their feelings on their sleeve.
- Compassionate leaders care for all human beings— friend or foe.

CHAPTER 17

"HEY, SIR. DO YOU REMEMBER THE TIME . . . ?"

JAMES "REV" JONES

"True compassion means not only feeling another's pain but also being moved to help relieve it." —Daniel Goleman

---

I ALWAYS ENJOY the opportunity to talk with some of the airmen I've worked with over the years, especially when they were a young member of a unit I'd commanded and are now a relatively senior officer or enlisted leader with significant levels of responsibility. After the normal pleasantries, the conversation tends to drift to the recounting of old war stories, often beginning with, "Do you remember the time that . . . ."

In those discussions, I've found it interesting to compare the events that I clearly remember to those the airmen in my organization recall. With great clarity, I remember major issues: the loss of an airman or aircraft, higher headquarters inspections, generating and employing airpower in combat, determining the fate of someone being tried under the Uniformed

Code of Military Justice, and the unit's capability to meet the mission in the toughest of environments and exceed the highest standards.

However, much of the day-to-day activity is cloudy, if I'm able to recall it at all. The airmen I spend time with tend to remember much more. Often, when their story starts with, "Do you remember," my embarrassed response is, "I might . . . but you'll have to remind me."

I recall talking with a relatively senior officer who had been a captain in one of the wings I commanded. Of all the things that happened during his tenure in the wing, he recalled the time he was trying to get accepted into the Weapons School. As part of that process, he asked to meet with me to discuss his application package and request my support—something I easily gave as he was one of our true superstars.

I provided a letter of recommendation, a required portion of the application package. Then, together, we hoped for the best. Unfortunately, I received word a few months later that he had not been accepted for that cycle—a common occurrence driven by limited class sizes and an extremely competitive selection process.

I walked down to the squadron to tell him the bad news, assured him there would be more opportunities, and encouraged him to keep trying. It was as simple as that. However, I learned in our later discussion that he was surprised that the *wing commander* would actually take time to come to the squadron and personally pass on the news.

I was as equally surprised, as that personal touch was what I'd seen from my commanders over the years. I certainly didn't see it as something special based on what I had observed. Based on the lessons learned from my previous commanders, *not* going to see him simply would have been wrong.

That's when I relearned the importance of knowing the people who work with you on a personal level and helping them through the tough times and disappointments we all face at one time or another. I can trace much of whatever success I might have had throughout my career to a number of superb leaders who did just that for me—and especially one brigadier general, whose compassion for my circumstances directly altered my leadership path through the Air Force.

After I had been medically disqualified from flying aircraft equipped with ejection seats, I was assigned to be the deputy operations group commander for the 552nd Air Control Wing, the home for the Air Force's Airborne Warning and Control System (AWACS). Other than benefiting from their battle management expertise during my years flying fighters, I had no experience in actually employing the system. As such, I was uneasy about taking on a supervisory role with my first immersion into their world.

I spent the first few months learning to fly the aircraft and gaining a basic understanding of the crew coordination required to perform the mission successfully. (The typical crew consists of four flight crew members plus thirteen to nineteen mission crew members, depending on the operational requirements.) I was scheduled to fly my first mission qualification training sortie on a previously innocuous date: September 11, 2001.

I never got airborne.

As we watched the attacks against the North and South Towers in the World Trade Center complex and learned of the fate of United Airlines Flight 93 at the Pentagon, the wing immediately shifted into an operational mission. We were to help protect the homeland by sanitizing the airspace, as the FAA had directed all commercial traffic to land. We would also provide battle management to military aircraft that had taken to the skies to defend against the potential of further attacks.

Even though I was new to the wing and the mission, I was called to the Wing Operations Center, the ops center that controlled AWACS. I was one of the Operations Group supervisors and thus part of the senior battle staff.

That became the focus of my life for the next seven months.

As Operation Enduring Freedom began in Afghanistan, the wing was directed to deploy a contingent of aircraft to the Middle East to support operations. The operations group commander deployed with them as the expeditionary wing commander for the deployed location, leaving me as the acting operations group commander as the wing continued to support Operation Noble Eagle, the ongoing defense of the homeland.

The 552nd wing commander was known to be blunt and direct. He demanded the highest levels of performance from those in his wing. Despite my lack of AWACS experience, he made it clear that he expected me to run operations effectively, and he subsequently fully empowered me to do so. While never explicitly stated, he also made it clear that my lack of experience was not going to be an acceptable excuse for not keeping up with the demands placed on the wing—and deservedly so.

With support and assistance from a number of true professionals within the Operations Group, we put plans and procedures together that enabled the wing to meet the nearly impossible tasks to support the increased security requirements for the homeland while simultaneously supporting operations in Afghanistan.

But, due to our hectic operational tempo, I'd completely lost track of the ongoing administrative activity that continued on pace, including the board process to select the next candidates to be selected as group commanders.

As a career pilot, I'd hoped to be selected as one of these candidates for a flying Operations Group.

However, one of the basic criteria required candidates to have a minimum of ninety flying hours in the mission category, whether fighter, bomber, command and control, etc. I'd barely been able to accrue the minimum number of required flight hours. My primary duties since 9/11 had forced me to be on the ground, ensuring operations continued to run smoothly. Plus, the vast majority of our daily flights were committed to operational missions with little room for the additional training I required to become a fully qualified mission pilot.

The board of senior officers that select candidates for Group Command is charged with producing a roster of the most qualified people for approval by the Major Command commander, a four-star general. In doing so, they rely heavily on the records available for review. As I had not been assigned to the 552nd ACW long enough to generate a performance report, they had no access to anything that described my performance at the wing. Coupled with my limited number of flight hours in command and control aircraft, they understandably did not place me on the flying Operations Group list. Rather, they recommended me for consideration as an air support operations group commander.

When the wing commander informed me of the board's recommendation, I was disappointed yet still grateful for the opportunity to continue to command. I resigned myself to the fact that I wouldn't have the opportunity to command a flying organization. I made the personal commitment to prepare as best I could for an ASOG command opportunity, and I returned to the task at hand of helping keep the AWACS operations on track.

However, my wing commander did not easily accept the board's recommendation. He took it upon himself to try to amend the list, an uncommon occurrence. As opposed to the Weapons School process that allows multiple opportunities to be selected, he knew this was a singular decision point that would determine my future.

He directly engaged with the commander of Air Combat Command, the Major Command that the 552nd ACW is assigned to, and explained the somewhat unique circumstances that had prevented my accrual of additional flight hours and the administrative constraints that had prevented the inclusion of a performance report covering my time at the wing. He approached the challenge of amending the group commander candidate list with the same tenacity and relentless drive he used in running the wing.

Consequently, he was eventually successful in getting me placed on the candidate list for a flying Operations Group. Within a matter of weeks, I was selected to command the 93rd Operations Group at Robins Air Force Base, which subsequently led to the opportunity to command *three* operational flying wings and ultimately advance to the general officer ranks.

It isn't lost on me that the AWACS wing commander could

have left well enough alone. After all, I'd made the cut to be an ASOG Commander, which provided me the opportunity to continue to lead within our Air Force. I have no idea what may have happened had that become the path I needed to follow.

I do know that my career as a senior officer within the Air Force is directly attributable to the personal commitment from Brigadier General Ben T. Robinson to resolve what he perceived to be an ill-informed decision by the selection board.

I don't know if, after sixteen years, General Robinson recalls the event as clearly as I do. But the next time I have the opportunity to see him, I'll start the conversation with, "Sir, do you remember the time that . . . ."

TAKEAWAYS

- Compassionate leaders really know the people they work with—not just their name.
- Compassionate leaders recognize that everyone struggles with life at one time or another, then they do all they can to assist.
- Compassionate leaders care more about the people in the organization than themselves.

CHAPTER 18

THE OTHER SIDE OF THE STORY

RICHARD "BEEF" HADDAD

"Leadership grows like tall trees. It needs both toughness and flexibility. Toughness for accountability, flexibility to adapt to changes with a compassionate and caring heart for self and others."
— Amit Ray

IN THE RESERVES, we talk about "the three-legged stool" of responsibility every airman stands on. Those three legs are their family, their primary job, and their Air Force Reserve duty. They must keep their balance distributed around that stool, giving equal attention and devotion to all three areas of responsibility.

It's a nearly impossible task.

As a leader, if I lack compassion for those in my command, one of those legs may collapse. Of course, a two-legged stool is going to topple over.

As a squadron commander, I deployed with the 711th

Special Operations Squadron on four occasions from 2001–2003, ranging from Iraq to Uzbekistan and back to Iraq. We were supporting combat operations with MC-130 Combat Talons. In all those deployments, I had a small support staff. We were given the precise number of service members to sustain and accomplish our particular missions. Consequently, whenever those numbers dwindled, the missions became much more difficult to manage.

Well, guess what. Those numbers dwindled every time.

One airman's relative was dying. Another airman was on the brink of divorce. Yet another had a child back home with an escalating drug problem. And that's only a sampling of the external issues that faced our squadron on a routine basis.

Because I was the squadron commander, it was my responsibility to accept or deny their requests to return home.

I recall one such instance that occurred during my time as vice commander of the Air Force Reserve Command.

One of our lieutenant colonels, who'd been an incredible fighter pilot, had tested positive for marijuana use. Drug use of any kind within the Air Force isn't condoned, and officers, in particular, are expected to maintain the highest standards and set an example.

Upon learning of his failed drug test, I was first inclined to throw him out of the Air Force. That's what our lawyers wanted me to do. It was also the easiest, fastest way to rectify the situation. We could not tolerate that kind of behavior, and I worried about the precedent it would set if I let him remain.

However, I knew I couldn't make a decision about his future until I'd heard his side of the story. As his leader, it was my job to hear him out.

I soon came to learn that he only had about a year and a half to serve in the Force before he could retire. I felt bad for his unfortunate timing and that he'd served nearly twenty years in the Force. But, to me, that alone wasn't an adequate reason to retain him. He'd violated one of our hard-and-fast rules.

But then he told me more.

He'd been having problems with his wife and teenager. I knew he was a family man, but I hadn't known about his home situation until then. I felt stirrings of compassion, knowing full well how much our "extra" jobs within the Air Force Reserve could place undue stress on a family.

Then he finally told me what had caused him to test positive for marijuana. He'd had intense back pain since his flying days, an unfortunately common issue for men and women who fly fighters. Flying fighters at speeds up to 1500 miles an hour places immense strain on their bodies and backs. That lingering, chronic pain had resulted in further problems, including worsening mental health. He'd been seeking psychological help from the Air Force but felt that he wasn't improving, mentally or physically. So he'd tried marijuana to help ease the pain that constantly coursed through his body and his mind.

I may have been a vice commander of the Air Force Reserve, but I'm not heartless.

I ordered a fine against his salary and gave him a letter of reprimand, but I allowed him to remain in the Air Force. Had I kicked him out, he wouldn't have had insurance to get the help he needed or a job to ensure that his problems at home didn't increase. And, of course, he would have lost the ability to retire and all its attendant benefits. By allowing him to stay on for the next year and a half, I helped ensure that his family was going to survive and that he could get the psychological and medical care he needed.

Ultimately, he received a medical retirement, and his

family matters are still intact. He has since expressed his grati-
tude to me for allowing him to continue his service so that he
could achieve retirement.

As a leader, if you lack compassion for those you lead, then you
don't deserve their loyalty and faithful service to your organization.

To prevent such a failure, get to know your people. You
need to know about the men and women whom you lead and
who serve alongside you. You don't have to delve into their
family histories, but you should know more about them than
just their job title and how their responsibilities relate to your
position. You need to know about them: about their families,
their problems, their plans, their hopes, their fears, etc.

In other words, you need to exercise compassion.

That way, when a colleague or subordinate seems off-kilter,
you've earned the right to ask what's really going on. And, more
often than not, they'll honestly tell you which leg of their stool
is about to give way.

During my tenure as a leader in the Air Force, I made it a
point to know my people and their families. I also ensured that
my supervisors and aircraft commanders knew *their* people and
their respective families. This cascade of compassion resulted
in colleagues who weren't afraid to approach me with their
subordinates' problems before those problems became large-
scale issues. The airmen on my team could tell me, "We have a
problem. Joe's wife is about ready to divorce him. He needs to
get back home."

I could trust their judgment, and they could trust mine. My
airmen knew I was tough but flexible.

So, what about you as a leader?

In any large, hierarchical organization with multiple layers of supervisors, from line production to vice presidents, the leader must not just set the example for compassionate leadership but must expect and reward compassion in supervisors at every level. Supervisors should be encouraged to pay close attention to the employees in their charge and ensure the lines of communication are always open.

In other words, you need to show your compassion and inject its value into your corporate culture.

For me, I knew I could trust the judgment of my supervisors and aircraft commanders, and they could trust mine. My airmen knew I was tough but flexible.

Had I been in my lieutenant colonel's shoes—had I been the man who'd tried marijuana as a last resort to dull the pain he'd endured for so long—I would have wanted tough but flexible leadership too.

In other words, I'd have wanted compassion.

TAKEAWAYS

- Compassionate leaders take the time to truly know their people.
- Compassionate leaders earn the right to ask tough questions of their subordinates.
- Compassionate leaders don't fear showing their compassion.

CHAPTER 19

RECTIFYING A COLOSSAL MISTAKE

TOM "HONEZ" JONES

> "It is critical to understand and appreciate the situations your airmen and their families find themselves facing. Sometimes these situations are of their own making; however, there are times when the individual is not responsible for the difficulty they face." —General (Ret) Bill Looney, USAF

IMAGINE you're an Air Force civilian (someone who works for the Air Force but isn't in uniform) and you've dutifully served your country for years.

On a day like any other, you receive an ordinary envelope in the mail. You open the envelope to find a single ordinary letter from the Air Force. On that letter, you scan the normal introductory lines until your eyes read this extraordinary line: "You can choose to pay your $100,000 debt by personal check or have it deducted from your monthly pay."

Incredulous, you reread the letter from the beginning, but

more slowly this time. Surely, you must have missed something. There's no way the Air Force is asking you to pay them back.

Right?

In 2013, this unfortunate circumstance befell dozens—if not up to one hundred—Air Force civilians under my charge as vice commander of the US Air Forces in Europe. Their "debt" ranged from tens of thousands to hundreds of thousands of dollars.

It probably doesn't need to be said, but the affected civilians were upset, confused, and hurt.

How did it happen?

These service members had been receiving money they were not legally entitled to due to a long-ago misinterpretation of a particular regulation. A legal decision in Washington, DC, had recently overturned that policy—a policy my organization had been following for decades.

Consequently, the money had to be repaid.

But what fault did the civilians have in this situation?

They were being suddenly saddled with immense debt for an issue they never knew was an issue—or could have ever become an issue.

The faceless system was running on autopilot. Compassion for the affected was nonexistent—until my team stepped in.

As soon as I'd heard about what was happening, I hosted a meeting with all of the affected civilians and their supervisors. Before any of them spoke, I could see fear and anger spread across their faces. When they spoke, I heard loud voices. Some cried. They felt helpless. I felt deep compassion for them.

But, as the general officer in the room, I was the in-person representation of the organization demanding repayment. I was "them," as if I'd been the one to write their letters. Consequently, gaining their trust required several meetings. Eventually, I convinced them that I understood their emotions, shared their discontent, and intended to fight on their behalf so that this corporate snafu wouldn't disrupt their lives so immensely.

About a month after our initial meeting, I once again gathered the affected workforce and laid out the timeline of events. I wanted everyone to be on the same page and to know exactly what had led to the decision that was affecting their finances. I also shared what I was going to do to help them and yet again promised my full support.

I back-briefed and enlisted the support of the USAFE commander, the Air Force chief of staff, the judge advocate general, and senior executives from the Defense Finance and Accounting Service. The commander was equally disturbed by the problem and supported my efforts on behalf of the command to rectify the problem.

I also engaged the bureaucracy back in Washington, both civilian and military, to drum up support for our cause. Through that long and arduous process, I realized that the farther removed you are from a problem and the people experiencing that problem's direct aftermath, the easier it is to act in a technical and dispassionate manner.

But I was on the front lines. I couldn't afford to be dispassionate with men and women I had to look in the eye.

Over the next year, I continued meeting with our workforce until we ultimately arrived at a solution that most considered satisfactory.

The workers were asked to sign a form acknowledging their respective "payments owed," and we made sure to include language that they were not signing a legal agreement that they had, indeed, collected the money incorrectly. The affected workers then applied for relief through a different accounting mechanism, essentially relieving them of the burden that had been inadvertently and suddenly placed upon them.

Not everyone was happy—it was a compromise, after all. But, to a person, they all expressed their appreciation that a senior leader had both listened to their pleas for help and had worked so diligently on their collective behalf.

Through that difficult challenge and the many similar ones I've faced during my Air Force career and my time as aviation director for the city of San Antonio, I learned a few things about compassionate leadership.

Understand and acknowledge the emotions involved in the situation at hand, but keep your emotions in check.

As the leader everyone was looking to for answers and assurance, the pressure I felt was intense and singularly focused. I learned that showing compassion during a crisis helps stabilize the situation. When the people around me seemed to lose their cool, I worked hard to keep mine.

Regardless of how bad the situation was (e.g., an aircraft accident, a fatality, an act of terrorism, massive budget shortfalls, etc.), I was determined to show empathy, project a calm demeanor, and force my staff to follow my lead. Once people calmed down, we could begin the hard business of figuring out the best way ahead.

That doesn't mean I wasn't inwardly ruffled or flustered, but I tried never to show that to the organization. I've seen organizations mirror the demeanor of their agitated, screaming leaders. Such a reaction by leadership only amplifies the uncertainty and turbulence that immediately follows any crisis.

Handling a stressful situation with compassion helps alleviate some of the angst of the situation and offers others a behavioral example that generates support for those facing the tough event. A leader can show compassion and still remain in charge.

Communicate up and down your chain of command.

I knew most of the people in Washington working on my earlier financial issue; they were good leaders. But I was disappointed by the slow movement to support our people. More than once, someone hid behind the non-answer answers of: "It's the law," "It's the rule," or "I can't change that." Then they'd fail to pursue any other options.

They were miles away from the affected population and had dozens of other pressing problems. However, I'm confident that, had they been facing these folks every day, listening to their stories and trying to calm their fears, they'd have acted differently—and more compassionately.

Fortunately, as I spoke with individuals higher up the ladder of leadership in the organizations I was dealing with, I found more reasonable and compassionate behavior. They focused their organizations' efforts into pursuing out-of-the-box solutions. Ultimately, we addressed the law and received legal relief from some of the restrictions.

While communicating our needs up the chain, I also made sure to communicate what was happening down the chain. I knew my organization would benefit from hearing my personal thoughts on the crisis. I also knew that I couldn't send a form letter. They needed to hear and see me in person. Had I not voiced what was happening, I feared the affected civilians would be subjected to swirling opinions and open speculation, which are rarely accurate.

So, I shared openly, honestly, and compassionately about what had happened, what was happening, and what I hoped would happen.

Compassion can't be allowed to overwhelm a leader's responsibility to lead their organization through the crisis.

Crises demand action for a resolution. But it's easy to become paralyzed in the quest for more information, or for more definitive information. The devastation caused by a crisis can also result in an inability to act.

But, as I learned so often, a leader will never have 100 percent of the information they need. Instead, they must learn to trust themselves and their team and make a decision.

Once I collected enough information to see a way forward, I made a choice and moved on it. I knew something had to change so that our organization could move forward and we could get back to normal operating procedures without a mountain of debt threatening to crush the morale of our Air Force civilians.

Leaders are generally placed in a position of past proven competence and sound judgment. Leading with compassion through a crisis offers any leader the opportunity to prove themselves yet again.

If there's fault to be had, own it.

I'm impressed by leaders who, rather than hide when

things go wrong, acknowledge responsibility for the mistake—even if that mistake wasn't theirs. I've come to learn that organizations are impressed by the same action.

The civilians in my example were furious at being portrayed as somehow being complicit in the bad interpretation of a financial regulation. But it was our fault for sending them a poorly worded document which made it appear that the problem was solely theirs to correct. We couldn't have offended them more if we'd tried.

However, once we apologized and started talking to them individually, we were able to forge a way ahead that satisfied them.

I'm confident that this was a byproduct of the compassionate approach we'd taken once the situation became known to leadership and the leadership shouldered the responsibility for the problem.

Manage expectations.

It's a natural reaction to tell everyone "It's going to be OK" as a means of tamping down uncertainty and alarm. I tried not to say that during a crisis unless I was confident I was right.

Instead, I offered a listening ear and a dogged determination to do my best to do right by my team. I relayed the problem, I told the affected members what I was going to do to address the problem, and I spoke about my desired outcome for all of us.

But, through all of those words, I had to manage my team's expectations. I was cautious not to promise a happy ending that might not be achievable. I tempered optimism with realism, but I always kept one ideal at the forefront: compassion.

After all, how would I have felt to open an ordinary letter

on a day like any other and be asked to pay back my employer for hundreds of thousands of dollars?

TAKEAWAYS

- Compassionate leaders listen to the needs of their subordinates.
- Compassionate leaders see problems through their teams' eyes.
- Compassionate leaders maintain their emotions.

CHAPTER 20

CARRY THE TORCH

ROB "MUMBLES" POLUMBO

"Compassion and tolerance are not a sign of weakness,
but a sign of strength." —Dalai Lama

"LOOK AROUND THE ROOM," our pilot training instructor ordered.

Dutifully, the fifty-one aspiring pilot candidates who comprised my training class in 1984 shifted their heads from side to side.

Our instructor continued, "Twenty-five percent of you selected for assignments in ejection-seat aircraft will eject and/or perish in accidents over your career. *Twenty-five percent!*"

I was caught so off guard that I failed to do the math to put this statistic into real perspective. I was shocked, too. *Surely that can't be true.* As his statement kept ringing through my ears throughout the rest of that day, the simple math revealed itself: one in four of my comrades will have a mishap that causes them to jump out of their aircraft or have an accident risking injury or death.

There's no way that can be true! my young and naive self thought.

In fact, at least for my training class, it wasn't true. The percentage turned out to be much higher. Of the twelve pilots who would go on to receive ejection-capable aircraft assignments (including me), *five* were eventually forced to eject from their aircraft. Three of the five perished as a result.

By the time I reached the end of my flying career, I could do the sobering math: 42 percent of my pilot training class comrades had fulfilled our instructor's morbid prediction. If not for the grace of God on two dire emergencies in my F-16 that luckily worked out in my favor during my four-thousand-hour career, I would have made that number 50 percent.

Death is our unfortunate yet ever-present, invisible copilot. Every airman is trained to understand the risks he or she must make on a daily basis in service to country. We nod shocked assent to the statistics our instructors try to bore into our heads, but the numbers seldom become real until we all experience losing a comrade.

On a cool November morning in 2002, flying a training mission over the Utah salt flats in preparation for deployment to Southwest Asia during the war in Iraq, one of my closest friends, Lieutenant Colonel Dillon "Mcfly" McFarland, crashed and died while flying a sortie in his F-16 Fighting Falcon aircraft. He was one of the nation's best and brightest of pilots. He was highly respected in the aviation ranks. But unforeseeable accidents can still happen to the best.

His beautiful wife and young children were devastated by

the loss, as was I. His commander enlisted the help of everyone on base to support the grieving family. Consequently, hundreds of airmen in the fighter community immediately came to the family's aid during that difficult time.

I was offered the great privilege of speaking at his memorial. Over five hundred people—some of whom had traveled from across the globe—came to pay their respects to our fallen brother and his family. I was overwhelmed at the turnout, even though I knew the caliber of the man we had lost. His memorial was yet another reminder to me of how our Air Force leadership placed great importance on developing a very close and compassionate family.

But the Air Force's care for this family didn't end when the memorial service concluded. The most astounding testament to our organization-wide compassion is that dedicated support for this man's family continues today. Out of this tragedy, a close-knit and inseparable group developed around his family and closest friends. For the past seventeen years, the family ties within this group have only become stronger, even crossing generational lines as our children's children now know and cherish each other. We continue to honor our friend through our community of compassion.

I realize that the outside world—those unfamiliar with what it's like to serve our country—don't understand the deep compassion that runs through our organization. They hear and see single-dimension portrayals of the military on TV, in the movies, and even in the news. But it's not until you're on the inside, experiencing the life of an airman, in both good times and tragically bad times, that you understand your family is much larger than you once thought.

Over decades of losses during both peacetime training and combat operations, I witnessed how the USAF leadership placed importance on instilling compassion in the ranks. *Every* airman *and* their families were necessary members of the team. No one would be left behind or forgotten.

I attended a memorial service in 2018 for an Air Force pilot, Colonel Peter Stewart, whose remains had been recently repatriated from the jungles of Vietnam. His aircraft had been shot down in 1966, and he'd been listed as Missing In Action ever since then. For over fifty years, his wife and children were forced to endure not knowing what had ultimately happened to their loved one. I'd grown up and gone to school with one of his sons. I saw firsthand how heavily this "not knowing" weighed on the family.

Their story was but one of thousands since the end of the US and Vietnam conflict. Due to the unfriendly terms at the end of the war, the Vietnamese government had prevented our government from searching for the thousands of soldiers, sailors, airmen, and marines who'd given their lives or were otherwise unaccounted for. Affected military families in the US had to endure the unenviable task of trying to find closure without the knowledge of what had happened, or even where their loved ones ultimately were.

Gratefully, friendlier relations between our governments have prevailed. As soon as it was possible to do so, our military services immediately expended vast resources and efforts to bring our fallen heroes home. To date, over a thousand service members have been repatriated. Many more remain unaccounted for, but the repatriation work continues.

While I was at Colonel Stewart's memorial service, I viewed his casket and saw the family's tears of sorrow mix with a knowing grimace of fulfillment. At least they now had some closure. And I again saw how an organization could show compassion. In fact, I'd heard that the Air Force chief of staff had personally contacted Colonel Stewart's wife to offer condolences on behalf of the entire Air Force family and a grateful nation. When I heard that, I was proud to be a member of a compassionate country and military service who vowed to leave no one behind—service members and family members included.

That broad compassion filters through the ranks. It has to in our line of work.

The bond between airmen is unique from other professions because there's inherent, mortal danger when hurling your body into the air at great speed with nothing more than a metal tube surrounding you.

Since the beginning of aviation, mankind has been enamored with "slipping the surly bonds of earth," even though a mistake or malfunction can quickly result in severe injury or death.[1] This courage to go where no one has gone before developed not only a spirit of ingenuity and innovation but also a special compassion for a fellow airman's bravery to risk everything in their efforts to conquer the unknown.

So, with such imminent death and destruction always riding shotgun, how can a leader inspire and motivate a group of airmen to continue to perform under such dangerous conditions? How does a leader, after knowing that his squadron has lost an airman, and knowing that his squadron is thinking about their own mortality as a result, encourage his men and women to keep risking their lives for their country?

The answer isn't as simple as I would like to think, but I know compassion plays an essential role. Our leaders understand the risks. They too have lost comrades all along the chain of command. They too have faced the same fears in the face of death. They know what it's like to face the uncertainty of training or combat missions, especially in the recent aftermath of having lost a fellow airman. So their compassion for those they lead is palpable.

As a young man in the early years of my career, I believed there was no room for compassion in our ranks. After all, our ultimate job was to deliver death from above. I didn't think we could afford to be compassionate because it would dull the edge I felt we all needed to accomplish our mission. I thought compassion was a sign of human frailty and weakness, which had no place in military service.

I was wrong.

As I matured as a leader, I came to understand and embrace compassion as our greatest strength. I became convinced, more than ever, that compassion is a key ingredient to leading others, especially when the mission presents a real and mortal danger. Compassion ensured that no tragedy, obstacle, or setback could ultimately deter our organization from success.

Through my decades-long career, I also witnessed how, for compassion to flow through the ranks, it must begin at the highest point: from the top leaders on down. Our Air Force leadership's determination to create a unified and compassionate family out of a disparate and diverse group is an essential aspect of keeping our teams focused on the mission while still maintaining support and care for our fallen airmen and their loved ones. The need for such top-down compassion can't be overstated, especially in a profession of arms that relies on citizen volunteerism to place service above self.

I believe every leader of every organization ought to create an environment of care and support for one another. Team members ought to find comfort in being treated with respect and truly feeling that they belong to a family, in good times and in bad. If you were to inspect the most successful organizations in business, academia, or public service, I guarantee that compassion is the cornerstone of their success.

And their leaders will be in front, carrying the torch.

TAKEAWAYS

- Compassionate leaders know their people *and* their families and leave no one behind.
- Compassionate leaders are empathetic to the needs of the team.
- Compassionate leaders create supportive, caring environments.

PART 5

CHARACTER

CHAPTER 21

MISSILE IMPACT

TOM "HONEZ" JONES

"That night was characterized by anger, impatience, and finally frustration on the part of the senior people in the White House and the Department of Defense. General Brown, instead of succumbing to all this, calmly discussed with me what steps must be taken in the future to insure no repeat of such an incident. He immediately knew we could not change this one, but we'd better be sure of the future." — Major General (Ret) William Shedd, US Army

---

ON MARCH 20, 2003, the first day of the war in Iraq, our warning system blared throughout my command center. Iraqi missiles were incoming—and fast.

Although we'd practiced this specific scenario dozens of times before the war had begun, I still wasn't prepared for the real-world shock of the alarm and what it actually signified. We were under attack. In ten minutes or less, our center could be decimated. Or chemical weapons could be dispersed. The risks were life-and-death—something that even consistent training can never quite prepare you for.

As a wing commander, I was in the command center trying to keep track of the hundreds of sorties being flown on the first day of Operation Iraqi Freedom, including the massive efforts to support our units. My mind was heavily preoccupied when the sirens blared.

Then, adding to the noise and instant chaos, our phones rang. My higher headquarters, located in Saudi Arabia, was calling to confirm the launch. As I answered the phone, I looked at the two young enlisted controllers who sat alongside me. Despite their training for this exact moment, they looked terrified.

A screen flashed the time to impact as three minutes and counting.

As calmly as I could, I instructed them to don their protective chemical warfare gear. This was policy since we never knew if an incoming missile had chemical warfare capabilities. It was better to be momentarily inconvenienced by putting on the restrictive equipment than to be wrong.

The men did as they were instructed while I sounded the alarm throughout the rest of the base.

The screen flashed one minute and counting.

In the chaos of that moment, I tried to put my gear on while continuing to answer phones and direct the rest of the battle staff. I wasn't totally successful. I'd only managed to place my gas mask over my head—the most important part, in my opinion—and one more article of protective gear before our countdown timer reached zero.

Missile impact.

The siren stopped.

So did all sound within the command center.

We didn't hear or feel an explosion, meaning that the missile had impacted some distance away from us. Our space-based tracking system displayed its best approximation of the missile's landing, but the missile's short time in flight made it impossible to receive a location with pinpoint accuracy. The missile had appeared to detonate about ten miles away from us.

After ascertaining that no chemical elements were in play, I ordered our men to remove their chem gear. By that point, the two controllers had composed themselves. For the remainder of that harrowing shift and throughout the rest of Operation Iraqi Freedom, which would include several more missile attacks, they provided superb support. In fact, they maintained perfect control and composure for all subsequent attacks.

I'd like to think that, having observed my actions under pressure, these men realized they could perform at a higher level as well. And the only reason I can say I showed character at that moment is that such character was modeled for me by many men and women in the Air Force.

I don't have the room to name them all or how they all affected my character development just by way of their lives and leadership, but one man tops my list of leaders with high character: the 20th Chief of Staff of the Air Force, General (Ret) Mark Welsh.

I had the good fortune to work for General Welsh on multiple occasions. He routinely provided inspirational leadership anchored by principled character—behavior that I internalized and attempted to duplicate as I rose in rank.

As Chief of Staff, General Welsh was confronted with problems of overwhelming magnitude on a daily basis. At nearly every hour, he was brought a new "unsolvable" problem.

On more than one occasion, I was the one bringing him those problems. Though the spectrum of challenges he faced was broad, his responses became predictable: calm, graceful, sometimes injected with wry humor, and ultimately leading to the right solution for these seemingly unsolvable issues. Additionally, I never saw him express anger or frustration—though I'm certain he felt those emotions.

To me, his deepest expression of his inward character was revealed when an Air Force problem became a national news story.

Air Force leaders, including me, advocated retiring our fleet of outdated A-10 aircraft so that we could modernize and recapitalize other fleets. But the government and the military disagreed, even berating us for the suggestion. Many higher-ups thought the A-10 was required to provide support for our ground forces, but we believed support could be provided just as effectively by F-16s and F-15Es. And, as usual, a certain level of politics was involved: politicians who had a base with A-10s in their state or district feared the possible detrimental economic impact of losing those jets.

Personally, I found it difficult even to entertain the uninformed—and often incorrect—comments that were being made within the criticisms of our plan. I couldn't see how they couldn't see what we saw.

Although these factions accused the Air Force—and, by extension, General Welsh himself—of malfeasance, he provided measured, respectful responses. (Something I'm sure I couldn't have done under the same circumstances.) During his Congressional hearings and other speaking engagements during this time, the men and women under his leadership witnessed powerful examples of character under pressure.

I knew then that if one man could withstand such scrutiny and pressure at the highest echelons of power with grace and dignity, I could learn to do the same. He was then, as he still is now, my model for leading from deep, abiding character.

One last story reveals how essential the need for character is up and down the chain of command.

When I was commanding an F-16 wing in Arizona, I was informed before dawn that an accident had just occurred: an F-16 had been damaged on the flight line. I rushed to the site and saw a vehicle wedged beneath an F-16's nose. Numerous vehicles were parked around the accident site, with at least a dozen individuals talking about what had just transpired. I was then told that a young female airman had apparently fallen asleep at the wheel after a long overnight security shift on the flight line.

I spied her in the back of a safety vehicle segregated from the crowd and made my way to her to hear her side of the story. Her look at my approach told me she was clearly afraid, likely from both what had just happened and the possibility of what was about to happen.

"Are you all right?" I inquired.

"Yes. Physically, I'm OK," she replied, somewhat meekly.

"You're lucky the aircraft didn't collapse onto the vehicle. You could have been crushed."

She nodded her head at my obvious statement.

But I wanted to ensure she understood the gravity of the situation. I continued. "What happened?"

Without hesitation, she replied, "I fell asleep while driving."

Now it was my turn to nod.

She continued. "My shift was almost over. I was thinking about the studying I needed to get done for my classes. Then I closed my eyes for just a second. Next thing I know, I was jolted awake by the sound of my car hitting that F-16. I'm so sorry, General Jones."

I nodded again. I had been informed that she had been taking college courses in her off time. It seemed to me she may have been taking on too much and her workloads had caught up to her. Still, I was impressed with her forthrightness. She could have lied, or at least not have told the whole truth. After all, she had been the only person in that car. She could have blamed being distracted by something. Instead, she set the blame squarely on her own weary shoulders.

I guided the apologetic airman to our safety folks so she could be taken to the hospital for a full evaluation. Then I phoned General Bill Looney, my four-star commander, to advise him of the situation.

His reaction provided another benchmark for leading with character.

General Looney calmly listened to my recitation of events. Then he asked a few clarifying questions to ensure he had all the facts. As a highly successful fighter wing commander earlier in his career, General Looney understood the ramifications of such an accident: the loss of a valuable asset, the breakdown in procedures we'd put in place to ensure accidents like that wouldn't happen, and the shock that such an incident could send through the unit. It may have been a slow-speed accident, but it was still an accident, and consequences had to occur.

However, General Looney also understood that people make mistakes. The blunder the young airman had made was likely unintentional, even the result of someone who'd overextended herself to "be better," the challenge that the Air Force issues to every airman. His initial reaction was the same as mine: appreciation that she had responded truthfully and with integrity when questioned about the accident.

Ultimately, he left the decision regarding consequences to me.

I hung up the phone with a deeper appreciation of General Looney's character and the qualities he wanted the airmen in his command to exemplify. He did not measure worth by externals; he chose to look more deeply into a situation to ensure he was considering all the facts before passing judgment—yet another valuable lesson for me.

Shortly thereafter, I called the airman's commander and ordered, "Let's look at non-punitive ways to correct this situation." He complied. The airman had to undergo retraining. Her career would continue uninterrupted by a reduction in rank or a monetary fine—two outcomes that many had expected to occur.

While I was initially disappointed by the mishap on my watch, General Looney's careful consideration of the event helped me appreciate the fact that I had a hardworking airman who erred on the side of truth and displayed great character in a trying moment of personal failure.

I needed more of those types of airmen, not fewer.

I remain grateful to have served with that airman, with General Looney, with General Welsh, with those two enlisted controllers in Iraq, and with so many more men and women in the Air Force. They all exuded character from deep within, and each of them taught me unique lessons that would bear upon my life and leadership forever onward.

TAKEAWAYS

- Leaders with character lead by example.
- Leaders with character tell the truth, even at personal cost.
- Leaders with character don't measure worth by externals.

CHAPTER 22

DEFINING CHARACTER

H. D. "JAKE" POLUMBO

> "Leadership is a potent combination of strategy and character, but if you must be without one, be without strategy." —General H. Norman Schwarzkopf

WHEN I CONSIDER what it means for a leader to have impeccable character, one image instantly springs to mind: General Joseph F. Dunford, Commander of the International Security Assistance Force, ISAF, in the early-morning twilight, leading a remembrance ceremony for a fallen soldier at Kandahar Airfield in southern Afghanistan.

Starting in mid-2012, we served together in Afghanistan for the better part of a year. General Dunford was the commander of ISAF, which included troops and resources supplied from forty-four NATO nations. I was the commander of the 9th Air and Space Expeditionary Task Force in Kabul, and I also served as the Deputy Commander for Air, United States Forces Afghanistan.

While there, I lived in two small shipping containers and worked about a block away, in a two-story, gray box of a building where I spent most of my time. A third point in my four-sided, well-worn path was a large yellow building built by the Russians decades ago, where I often saw the general hard at work during meetings in his office or in a large conference room with his international staff. Our busy paths would cross by necessity and by chance, but it wasn't until he invited me to a memorial ceremony—a.k.a. a "ramp ceremony" in our military parlance—that I truly got to know the man.

If you would have traced my walking paths for my typical week in Kabul, you would have seen a small and consistent rectangle, including my fourth regular stop on the path, the chow hall. But, as commander of all US airmen, and many of the NATO airmen, in Afghanistan, I also spent a lot of time moving around the area of operation. I primarily traveled by helicopter, though I'd sometimes be taken by small aircraft. At other times, I would move as part of a two-SUV convoy with a security detail of up to four well-trained service members who became part of my "family" in the combat zone.

But, as you might imagine, my travel requirements paled in comparison to General Dunford's schedule. He traveled via a ten-passenger jet to get where he was needed, whether that was Qatar, the United Arab Emirates, back to NATO headquarters in Brussels, or even sometimes to Washington DC. And he always traveled with a full security detail and a capable, well-equipped communications team.

When he asked me to fly with him to attend a ramp ceremony at Kandahar Airfield, about three hundred miles south of Kabul, I dutifully accepted his invitation. Not only was I honored to pay my respects to our fallen soldier and travel with the commander, but I was also glad for the opportunity to talk one-on-one with the ISAF commander and ultimately to visit

Kandahar. That air base and the 451st Air Expeditionary Wing on the base were under my command for the year I was in Afghanistan. I traveled to the airbase regularly to visit our great airmen and speak directly with the wing commander—who happened to be a good friend as well.

I even spent Christmas that year at Kandahar with my oldest son, Captain Chad Polumbo, who would complete two deployments to Afghanistan in the first few years of his Air Force career.

On that day, the general and I helicoptered to Kabul International Airport, then boarded his jet for Kandahar. I had flown this route many times by now, but this particular trip was somber. We knew what we were about to do—yet again—since it was something none of us ever wanted to do: say good-bye to a brother-in-arms and try to say something helpful to the troops who had lost yet another friend and warrior.

We would pay our respects, give him a dignified sendoff, and get his remains back to his family in the states for repatriation as soon as possible. The U.S. Air Force had committed to move a fallen warrior with the highest priority no matter when the tragedy occurred. It was an important and sad mission to be assigned as the aircrew for this mission, but these aviators knew how critical it was to the troops who had to continue the fight the next day. I imagine that General Dunford was composing his thoughts for what he would say at the ceremony, so I let him ride in silence as I looked out the window at the familiar and rugged terrain below.

Once we arrived at the air base and the ceremony began late that night, General Dunford spoke eloquently and respectfully about the lost soldier. Then, members who'd known the fallen warrior walked up the ramp and into the huge C-17 cargo plane, where the casket had been placed. Each supervisor, peer, or subordinate spent just a few seconds saying goodbye to their fallen comrade. Some left coins or mementos on the casket, which would be collected and given to the family when the body arrived back at Dover Air Force Base in Delaware.

To say the proper things in the right way at the right time at such a service—and all without losing composure—is a true test of a leader's character. General Dunford was a master at this, and his words at that late-night remembrance service revealed why he is still such a great leader.

But my lesson in character development didn't end when the ramp ceremony concluded.

Just after midnight, General Dunford, his security team, his comm team, and I boarded the jet and headed back to Kabul. I was tired from the long day and emotionally drained from the ceremony. I thought the general would be too, and I assumed he'd want to get a few minutes of rest while on the plane, and I wouldn't have blamed him had he chosen to do so. I knew how much I coveted a little extra sleep in those busy days. Given his nonstop and chaotic schedule, I even imagined that he looked forward to his eventual rotation home to the states and a reunion with his family at some point, but since we all embraced the concept of service before self in these difficult wartime conditions, that thought rapidly slipped out of my mind.

However, I was truly surprised when the general engaged me in conversation during the flight back to Kabul International Airport. It wasn't just idle talk either. He asked about my thoughts on how the war would end and how the

Afghan people would survive the terrible scourge brought on by the Taliban. We also talked about opening new airfields and closing others that were too difficult to defend, even if the Afghan National Security Force personnel were still operating on the installation. We went over the new equipment inbound for the Afghan Air Force: helicopters and airplanes that would be difficult for the airmen and technicians to master. We discussed necessary logistics and air support for the troops, and, finally, the high degree of difficulty involved in teaching the Afghan Air Force how to conduct close air support in the challenging combat operations ongoing in General Dunford's area of responsibility. Our conversation ended just as our wheels hit the runway.

As I reflect on that night, I realize that the general had forgone rest so he could gather as much information from his subordinate commander as he could on that short flight. He also wanted to maximize his time by strengthening our relationship. This, of course, increased his standing in my eyes, from an already high level. Through his impressive words at the ramp ceremony and consideration for my opinions, I learned even more about his character, his composure, and his inner strength. From the ramp service to our conversation, his humanity and humility were even more evident, and I knew his concern for his troops was genuine and his sadness for our fallen soldier was profound.

I also had the opportunity to know and witness General Dunford's great moral strength. On Sundays, we would attend Mass together, either at the chapel at Kabul or at the Italian Embassy, where we were invited to attend the service as senior leaders for ISAF by a distinguished Catholic priest from Italy.

Based on these routine events and seeing his integrity in action, I came to understand that General Dunford attributed his own moral strength and robust character to his faith.

A consummate military leader, the general never let his guard down. I never saw him angered in meetings. He was *always* composed, the kind of man you would gladly follow into battle—or to a ramp ceremony. Every day that I worked for him, his character truly showed.

I opened this story with words from General Schwarzkopf: "Leadership is a potent combination of strategy and character." General Dunford had both. He could do strategy at the grand level, but he had character and moral conviction at every other level, in all of his daily activities. I was glad to have had him as my commander.

Unsurprisingly to me, my boss in Afghanistan was eventually called to a higher post. On October 1, 2015, General Joseph F. Dunford, Jr. became the 19th Chairman of the Joint Chiefs of Staff. He is the principal military advisor to the National Security Council, the secretary of defense, and the president.

TAKEAWAYS

- Leaders with character always honor the sacrifices of their followers.
- Leaders with character listen intently to their subordinates and value their opinions.
- Leaders with character develop and display moral strength under difficult circumstances.

CHAPTER 23

FIRED

RICHARD "BEEF" HADDAD

"Any fool can criticize, condemn, and complain, and most fools do, but it takes character and self-control to be understanding and forgiving." —Dale Carnegie

---

I GENERALLY DON'T TELL the following story because it's embarrassing.

In 2001, I was the commander of an MC-130 squadron. The Talon, as the multitasking plane is called, is a penetrating tanker that can go beyond enemy lines, refuel helicopters, and drop both supplies and Special Forces units. The MC-130s are workhorses for all sorts of special operations missions.

For the US invasion of Afghanistan in that year, I was chosen to lead the Talon effort with five planes and eight crews. Our missions were tasking and stressful, but our crews demonstrated their abilities above expectations. In fact, Army helicopter pilots knew that "Beef's guys" would always be there when needed. We accomplished our missions, and I thought I had capably performed my duties.

So, I was shocked when I wasn't chosen to command our next major operation: invading Iraq in 2003. Active Duty leadership had chosen one of their own to run the next phase. (I was in the Reserves at the time.) Why did their choice matter?

My squadron from 2001 had been an active associate organization, meaning that it was comprised of both active duty and reserve units. The reservists owned and maintained the aircraft; both the reservists and the active duty members flew the planes. We were operationally divided, even with separate chains of command—which made for interesting planning sessions, to say the least.

I would have internally agreed to leadership's decision if they'd had the preponderance of the force, but they didn't. We owned the planes, and I had the majority of the personnel. Consequently, the preponderance of the force was going to be reservists, just as it had been in the previous engagement.

However, I outwardly accepted the decision—but I still wasn't going to allow my crews to be deployed without someone to watch out for their best interests. So, I volunteered to be a deputy to the commander, who, coincidentally, had been *my* deputy during the invasion of Afghanistan. We have formed a great working relationship since 2001, but it was odd for me to be working for the man who had previously worked for me.

To be honest, I wasn't used to being second on the bench.

In my voluntary role, I sought to ensure equity for my crew in terms of mission steps and leadership opportunities. Essentially, I wanted them to be taken care of in every way possible.

As we conducted operations in Iraq, our missions seemed to go well. We were controlling the skies and had achieved air superiority. We controlled the Baghdad airport, established a tent city there, and even had a base exchange for our forces, where they could buy amenities. The threats we had first faced upon our arrival had significantly lessened.

But threats come in all forms while serving in the Air Force.

While I was conducting in-flight training over Baghdad, my satellite radio crackled to life. After having flown on a mission to Kirkuk, a crew of mine was on a return flight to Kuwait. They were in dire trouble. Their plane was on fire. A coolant system leak had allowed its glycol solution to ignite, resulting in a severe fire on the right side of the plane.

That aircraft's commander had been an airline pilot in his civilian career. Fortunately, for his team and himself, he'd just had his recurrent training, and one of the issues he'd covered was how to land a plane on fire. Based on a tragic example of a Swiss plane that had delayed its landing due to an onboard fire, in which all of its members were killed in the subsequent crash, the commander knew he had to land the plane as soon as possible. Based on their location at the time of the fire, the commander knew he would have to land in Baghdad ASAP.

The men within the aircraft fought to stifle the flames but to no avail. The fire wasn't abating. They also suffered from inhaling toxic fumes before being able to don their oxygen masks. Amazingly, the plane landed in Baghdad.

When we knew all the men were safe, we completed our mission, which only required a few more minutes, then we diverted our plane to Baghdad to check on our men.

They looked and acted like zombies, half-aware of what had just transpired and how close they had come to death. I imagine that many of them were thinking, *We come halfway across the world, not to be killed by enemy fire, but to be killed by a random fire?* I made these men immediately see a flight surgeon to ensure their continued safety.

While they were getting examined, I cautiously approached the colonel who'd recently taken over our operations. In fact, he'd been on the flight on fire. At the time, I was a lieutenant colonel who prided himself on taking care of his crew, but I also respected the chain of command. I knew I would have to discuss the situation with him carefully. I didn't know this colonel very well. Maybe that's why our conversation felt awkward and cumbersome. I typically have no problems communicating with anyone—but this time was different.

I requested that our men be sent back to Kuwait.

He replied that the entire crew needed to stay put.

I argued that we couldn't know how long the plane would be broken. It could take maintenance weeks or even months to fix.

He retorted that the crew needed to stay in the event that the plane would need to be flown out at a moment's notice.

I asked if he knew that the flight surgeon had just DNIFed the crew for at least twenty-four hours, if not longer. (DNIF means "Duty Not Including Flying".)

He insisted that the men stay.

I couldn't understand his reasoning. Though I didn't show it—as far as I know—I was angered by his decision. So, I made a command decision of my own.

The men would be sent back to Kuwait. Not only had they

barely survived a harrowing in-flight accident, but they'd also been serving for more than 110 days. They were weary and DNIFed. Plus, no one knew how long their plane would be grounded.

In my attempt at compromise, I mandated that the crew chief, the aircraft commander, and I would stay in Baghdad to fly the plane out if it could be resurrected in fairly short order—even though it would be illegal to fly as a three-person team. However, I also thought it highly unlikely that the plane would be getting off of the ground anytime soon.

I sent the rest of the crew home on my plane, knowing that I could get a crew back in time if necessary. We waited in Baghdad for three days before maintenance fixed the problem. However, when my plane landed in Kuwait, the colonel saw the flight engineer of the downed plane disembark from the plane I should have been on.

The colonel shouted, "Why are you here?"

The engineer could only reply with the truth: "Because Colonel Haddad told us to go home."

The reverberations of that singular moment quickly reached my tent in Baghdad. I received word that I was being relieved of my duties as commander of the 711 Special Operation Squadron due to my insubordinate actions.

I couldn't believe it.

I'd been leading that squadron for two years and had successfully led troops into combat. By that point, our squadron was the most highly decorated organization in the Air Force Reserve. We'd done incredible work, and I had thought I'd been an instrumental part of that.

Once back in Kuwait, I sought out the commander. He wasn't interested in hearing my perspective. As I was then slated to be heading home in a few days, I was restricted from both flying and being the volunteer deputy. Consequently, I went back to the States. Despite a pretty flawless track record, I wasn't given the opportunity to explain myself to my wing commander. I wasn't even granted a "fini flight," a major event of any Air Force flying organization where the departing airman, after their final flight, is usually met by the fire department and soaked with water and champagne when getting off the aircraft.

I collected my things from my office and drove home, not knowing what my future would hold.

"Your character defines who you are by the actions you take."[1]

If that's true, I rest assured that I took what I knew to be the right course of action despite its immediate cost to my career. In the aftermath of my dismissal, I could have easily raised all sorts of Cain, venting to anyone who would listen about my rightness and leadership's wrongness. But the voices of many mentors and friends outweighed my desire for justice. Instead of falling on my sword and retiring as a lieutenant colonel, I chose the high road.

Had that moment been the end of my Air Force career, I know I could have looked at myself in the mirror and been content with my service—including the decision that led to my departure. But those around me, with few exceptions, knew I had done the right thing. Much of the leadership within the Air Force Reserves got wind of the story.

Consequently, doors opened for me, including one that led to me becoming an Individual Mobilization Augmentee, i.e., a part-time reservist who works in an active duty organization, at Scott Air Force Base, Air Mobility Command. This new position was probably the best move to ever happen to me as it got me out of the Special Ops arena I'd been in for eighteen years, allowed me to expand my professional horizons, and granted me further opportunities to demonstrate what kind of leader I am.

Consequently, thirteen years later, I honorably completed my thirty-five-year career in the Air Force and retired as a major general.

Character matters. Now, I'm not saying you should go rock the boat with senior leadership to prove your character. But, if you feel strongly enough that what you're doing is right, that's the direction you should go. My character—a combination of my genes, education, and military training, as well as exemplary peers and mentors—won the day when I chose to move forward from that fateful incident in Kuwait.

If you hold your head up high, move forward, and allow your merits to be judged based on the good you have done for your nation and humankind, you will experience success—even after apparent failure.

TAKEAWAYS

- Leaders with character lead their teams well, even at the expense of professional loss.
- Leaders with character stand up for their team members.
- Leaders with character keep moving forward, trusting that their character will overcome any setbacks.

CHAPTER 24

THE KEY TO WILLING FOLLOWERSHIP

JAMES "REV" JONES

"Goodness is about character—integrity, honesty, kindness, generosity, moral courage, and the like. More than anything else, it is about how we treat other people." —Dennis Prager

---

IN 1990, I was a young captain, an experienced instructor pilot, a graduate of the USAF Weapons School, and very comfortable in the tactical arena. I was flying in a four-ship of instructor pilots conducting a training mission that included a low-level ingress (five hundred feet above the ground) to a controlled range to expend live munitions—the type of training missions we all lived for.

During the low-level portion of the flight, we had to make a 90-degree tactical turn from west to south—a maneuver that required me to fly underneath my wingman to cross from his left side to his right. As I passed beneath him, it felt as if someone had thrown a bowling ball down the intake of my engine.

I heard a loud bang—which is generally never good in a single-engine aircraft—and the airplane shook so hard it knocked my feet off the rudder pedals.

At the same time, the normal sounds within the cockpit were replaced by the strident WARNING and CAUTION tones of the aural warning system that is designed to call attention to the fault panels located within the cockpit, which, at the time, were lit up like the Christmas tree at Rockefeller Center.

This is also generally not a good thing in a single-engine aircraft.

After a quick scan of the engine instruments, it was obvious that the engine had failed. After executing the prescribed critical action procedures, it became even more obvious to me that the engine would not restart—leaving ejection as my only option.

Except for a minor parachute malfunction, the ejection itself was a relatively routine event, though I had a contusion on my jaw and cuts on my neck that appeared to be related to the parachute malfunction. I was able to contact the rest of my flight members with the survival radio I had access to, so they knew I was in a generally good condition. I was picked up relatively quickly and transported to the base hospital for further evaluation.

While not my best day, it certainly could have been worse. However, it was also the beginning of one of my most memorable leadership lessons.

My commander at the time of my most harrowing flight was a good person who faced the difficult challenge of dealing with a significant event early in his command tenure as he was still gaining experience leading at the organizational level. When we drove to work that morning, neither of us anticipated the challenges we'd both have to face.

The squadron is the Air Force's basic fighting unit, and flying squadrons are typically led by a lieutenant colonel, i.e., an officer who has been commissioned for fifteen to sixteen years. While these officers have been in supervisory positions throughout the years, squadron command is the first opportunity to truly lead an entire organization and be solely responsible for its success or failure. With command comes the requisite levels of authority to effectively lead the organization. However, while the authorities are automatically granted upon assumption of command, leadership skills are developed and refined over time. Therefore, there is a distinct difference between the two.

Yes, people in formal leadership roles have some modicum of authority to provide direction, establish policies, compel behavior, make decisions that impact the overall organization, and accomplish myriad other tasks. However, there are essential character traits I've observed in leaders over the years that enable *willing* followership, as opposed to the compulsory followership driven by authority alone. The most common elements include personal integrity, transparency in decision-making, establishing a foundation of trust with subordinates, and putting the organization above any personal interests.

With rare exception, the people I worked with and for during my thirty-plus years in uniform displayed these positive character traits on a daily basis. As a result, the people in the organizations they led were highly motivated, worked together to bring the unit to its highest levels of effectiveness, and had an esprit de corps that made them want to come to work each and every day.

However, I also acknowledge that the standard military unit will serve well even without strong leadership (as long as it's not toxic) simply due to the individual commitment to service above self that most people in our all-volunteer force possess. In my three decades of military service, I've had the opportunity to observe leaders in multiple stages of their development, and I've taken lessons from them all.

Leadership is definitely a learned skill, and it's unlikely every person placed in a new leadership position knows "all there is to know" on Day One. I certainly did not. The day I ejected from an F-16, my commander had the unfortunate responsibility of dealing with one of the most significant events a flying squadron commander has to face, and the first time you do so is a steep learning curve, to say the least.

Even though you may have thought about how you would handle such an event, when it actually occurs, the first few hours can be chaotic and confusing, and the unit's senior leadership has to quickly get things under control. While some procedural steps must take place, some instinctive decisions must often be made as well—and that can be harder than it sounds.

The people in the squadron were aware of the ejection event shortly after it occurred and that I was fine and in contact with the remaining flight members. One of my squadron mates offered to pick up his wife, drive to my house to pick up my wife and kids, and then bring them to the hospital to meet me. However, my commander (who was, again, fairly new to the position) elected to take a different course of action—one that was a little more formal.

He locked down all communication from the squadron (a normal procedure) and elected to go to my house himself, along with the flight surgeon and a chaplain. While I'm sure he felt that this was the proper procedure and he had the best of intentions, that particular threesome is generally reserved for casualty notifications—something every fighter pilot's spouse is well aware of.

When my wife opened the door and saw "the terrible trio," she immediately assumed the worst, and rightfully so. After they calmed her down and explained that, although I had ejected, I was all right, she remained confused (and slightly angry, to be honest) as to why they had chosen that particular notification method. When I'd heard what they'd done, I was just as confused (and slightly angry) as well.

I'm sure it's an experience she'll never forget.

After spending the night in the hospital, I was discharged and sent home to recover. For the next three days, I had no contact with anyone from my squadron—something I wasn't expecting as part of "the process." During that period, I had more than ample time to replay the event over and over in my mind.

I slowly started doubting myself.

I began to wonder if I'd misread the engine instruments in the heat of the moment and the engine had only stalled instead of completely failed. And if I'd performed the engine restart procedures incorrectly, which prevented a successful recovery. Which ultimately made me wonder if I were responsible for the loss of a $20-million aircraft.

Why else would my squadron have left me isolated for so long after such a traumatic event?

When I was finally called in to provide testimony to support the investigative process already underway to determine the cause or causes of the mishap, I had convinced myself I had been at fault in some manner. The senior officer leading the investigation called me over, asked if I were OK, and let me know what they had determined to date—which immediately alleviated my concerns. He also seemed as surprised as I was that no one had talked to me since the crash.

While it is the investigative board's responsibility to thoroughly investigate every aspect of such mishaps, I subsequently learned that my commander had also placed several calls to the Weapons School to gain assurance that the tactics we had employed were valid. In addition, he researched the administrative actions we had taken as a flight to ensure we had followed proper procedures in scheduling and flying that particular low-level route. None of those issues could have been a proximate cause to the mishap.

Consequently, right or wrong, my perception was that he did not trust me as an instructor and Weapons School graduate. It appeared he was concerned that anything we might have done wrong could be seen as a negative reflection against him personally.

During my remaining time in the squadron, I continued to give my commander due respect based on his position of authority. I worked to ensure I earned his trust, as my impression was that I had not done so before—for whatever reason.

While our commander was certainly effective in leading our unit, I'm confident that he wished he had been better prepared when he first received word of the crash. Why? Because I wished I had been better prepared when I lost my first aircraft as a commander.

Admittedly, I did not keep track of his Air Force career after I left the squadron. Leadership is a learned skill, and I hope he was able to continue to grow as a leader in any future command assignments through the experiences he gained in this isolated event.

I know I certainly did.

· · ·

TAKEAWAYS

- Leaders with character enable willing followership.
- Leaders with character display integrity, honesty, moral courage, and transparency, which lead to trust.
- Leaders with character know that the value of mutual trust within an organization cannot be easily measured but is readily observed.

CHAPTER 25

NEVER FORGET WHERE YOU CAME FROM

ROB "MUMBLES" POLUMBO

"Goodness is about character—integrity, honesty, kindness, generosity, moral courage, and the like. More than anything else, it is about how we treat other people." —Dennis Prager

---

I BELIEVE CHARACTER—MORE so than competence, courage, commitment, or compassion—truly separates great leaders from the rest of the pack.

Aspiring leaders can achieve success while exhibiting one or two of those qualities, but, without character, their successes will be short-lived. A seasoned leader steeped in character will have all the other attributes mastered, and his or her team will thrive in any environment or situation.

Ironically enough, developing character in a leader begins where you might least expect: in following. As a young fighter pilot, I remember the emphasis the unit placed on being a good wingman, a term synonymous with being a good follower.

Every responsibility of a wingman was directly related to supporting his flight leader and their mission objectives. Following was essential. The greatest leaders I've had were also the best wingmen.

In fighter-pilot terms, I'd define *followership of a wingman* as "Be on time, in formation, serve the mission, and support your leader!" It became a way of life and a badge of honor to be a good wingman. The pilots who embodied these skills the fastest were trained to become flight leaders well before their peers. It was a prestigious move up to the flight lead ranks.

However, this upward movement affected individuals in very different ways. Some took this advancement as a rite of passage that gave them the authority to disregard the principles that had brought them to the cusp of leadership. Others shouldered their new leadership responsibilities without losing sight of what had gotten them into that position in the first place.

The most toxic units I served in the Air Force were primarily the result of poor leadership. The leader had forgotten or disregarded the skills, lessons, and humble beginnings of being a follower. They forgot to stay in the books, to pay attention to the details, and how to act with integrity and excellence in everything they did. They stopped being part of the team and became self-serving. They ceased developing respectful lines of communication and relationships with their peers and subordinates.

Ultimately, they forgot where they had come from.

On the other hand, the greatest leaders I had the privilege to serve were exactly the opposite. At each higher level they attained, they pursued their followership skills with even greater passion. They not only knew their jobs but also became familiar with everyone's responsibilities on their respective team. They developed robust relationships up, down, and sideways throughout the organization. Over all individual desires, they put their teams and their missions first. But, most of all, they remained humble and approachable to their most junior members. They genuinely cared about everyone in the unit and their families.

One such individual immediately comes to mind when I look back on my thirty-three-year career in the military. I had the fortunate opportunity to know General Tod Wolters throughout my years in uniform, from as far back as my days at the Air Force Academy, when I overlapped his final two years at the zoo. He epitomizes character in every facet of his life and remains my greatest role model for how to lead.

General Wolters was a leader who never forgot he was a wingman first.

My first interaction with General Wolters came when he was assigned to the F-15 Fighter Weapons School division in the early 1990s. I had the pleasure to fly with him on a number of combat-training missions. He was a consummate professional aviator in every regard, from his meticulous planning and precise execution of the game plan to his thorough analysis of the mission results.

What impressed me the most were his objective and honest evaluations of his own performance and his interpersonal skills of relaying objective critiques of his teammates' performances. He was always the voice of reason and a peacemaker in resolving heated, high-ego confrontations with spirited fighter pilots. His objective was always to make the team even better before the next mission. This ability to bring opposing opinions to resounding consensus made him one of the most respected fighter pilots of our era.

During his time at this assignment, the Air Force made significant changes to the premier school, which caused turbulence in the fighter community. For decades, the Weapons School had been categorized as an elitist, non-inclusive club for fighter pilots that had alienated it from the rest of the force. Because of his foundation in humility, accountability, and credibility, General Wolters embraced the change to open the Weapons School to other operational communities to include bombers, search and rescue, and space forces. He knew this change would make our Air Force more combat capable, and he was a compelling advocate for its implementation. As a result, the school has now grown to twenty-one squadrons teaching twenty-four combat specialties at nine different locations. The motto of the graduates is "humble, approachable, credible."

With his credentials in followership firmly established, his journey continued through the field-grade ranks and command positions. His competence in the fighter community remained second to none. His commitment to the service was peerless. And his foundation remained firmly established in where he'd come from. His diversity of assignments, from aide-de-camp to commander, broadened his view of the entire Air Force, which led to a better perspective on how to best serve the airmen and civilians under his watch.

With each subsequent assignment elevating him further from his tactical roots, he remained grounded with those who made mission success possible. His watchful eye was not directed at his next promotion but rather on how he could improve the team's performance and advance those around him. Although we were not stationed at the same locations during this timeframe, I watched his progression from afar and received periodic feedback that confirmed my earlier impression of his selfless professionalism.

With a couple of general officer assignments behind me, I was selected to be his assistant at 12th Air Force headquarters in Tucson, Arizona, in 2014. He was the commander responsible for over five hundred aircraft and forty thousand airmen and civilian employees. At the time, I was going through a very difficult period of my career and had truly lost faith in my chain of command. I now had the great opportunity to personally view the polished product of a leader of character.

The assignment with him was truly a rebirth for me to recover lost character in my own life. Over a number of years of adversity, I had lost focus on what it meant to serve something greater than oneself. I had become immersed in self-pity and self-centeredness. I had lost my commitment to selfless service. Although it was never discussed, I am now convinced that my selection to serve as his assistant was not an accident but rather his personal decision to return me to the fold.

Through his powerful example of character, he silently reminded me of the vows I'd signed onto thirty years earlier. As I reflect on the many situations where I stood by his side, I remember my introspective thought of how far he had advanced in character development while I had stagnated.

The most indelible memory of his interpersonal skills was how he could enter a room filled with individuals from every level of the team and make every one of them feel as though they were the most important person in the room. He listened intently and unabatedly to everyone who engaged in discussion. His inspiration, positive attitude, and respect for every member of his team were compelling.

Even more telling, I never witnessed him ill-tempered, impatient, or in a fit of anger. His calmness under fire and good-natured demeanor were contagious. The year working at his side was instrumental in refreshing my memory of what it means to be a leader of character and helped to get my own journey back on track.

With my situation still not rectified, he compassionately took me along on his next assignment to the Pentagon. I was amazed at the ease of his transition to now be responsible for the entire Air Force process of organizing, training, and equipping the multi-mission force of over 460,000 individuals. He accomplished this first by using his followership skills of tedious after-work-hours effort to become a subject matter expert in the key processes of his job. He then melded into the framework of the system and built immediate relationships with the team. He was humble and approachable to his peers and subordinates and loyal to his chain of command—just as he had done thirty years earlier as a lieutenant. He had made it a point to bring everything he had ever learned with him.

Much more personally, I will never forget his courage, commitment, and compassion to support my family and me through a bitter battle with the Air Force. When most had abandoned us because it could have impacted their career, he took it as a personal mission, without regard for his future, to stand up and rectify the situation. Expending his valuable time and effort, he singlehandedly coordinated a resolution to allow me to finally retire with honor from the Air Force. Our paths soon diverged thereafter with my retirement and his promotion to four-star general with an assignment as the Commander of US Air Forces Europe. One thing that will never diverge from our journey together is his first-rate example as a leader of character.

By the time this book is published, I believe the president of the United States will have appointed General Wolters to an even higher position of responsibility. Many may say his selection resulted from his outstanding performance in his numerous general officer assignments.

I'll contend he was selected because he never forgot where he came from.

TAKEAWAYS

- Leaders of character are also the best followers.
- Leaders of character are humble, approachable, and credible.
- Leaders of character never forget their humble beginnings.

PART 6

ABOUT THE
AUTHORS

H. D. "JAKE" POLUMBO

MAJOR GENERAL (RET)

Major General (Ret) H. D. "Jake" Polumbo is a founding partner and senior consultant for Two Blue Aces, a leadership consultancy that specializes in strategic reviews, business plan development, and leadership and mentor training. His primary focus is in the defense and aerospace sectors, with an emphasis on leadership and business networking.

In 2015, after thirty-four years of service, Jake retired from the Air Force as the commander of the Ninth Air Force in South Carolina, comprising eight active-duty wings in the southeastern United States with more than 450 aircraft and over twenty-nine thousand active-duty and civilian personnel.

He entered active duty as a graduate of the U.S. Air Force Academy in 1981 and commanded at the squadron, group, and three times at the wing level. He served in strategic planning positions in Europe as the director of strategy and plans at U.S. Africa Command and in the Pentagon as the assistant deputy director for Global Operations on the Joint Staff. General Polumbo also served as a task force commander in Afghanistan in 2012. He attended the Federal Executive Institute and was a Senior Fellow at Georgetown University's Institute for the Study of Diplomacy.

An accomplished command pilot, Jake logged over three thousand flying hours in all models of the F-16, and he holds the distinction as the first and only Air Force general officer to fly the U-2 in combat, completing twenty-one missions in Operations Enduring Freedom and Iraqi Freedom.

Jake serves on the boards of the Central Florida Development Council and the Business School at Hawaii Pacific University. He also volunteers for his church in Lakeland in various capacities. He and his wife Sandra are Florida natives and have been married for thirty-eight years. Their oldest son, Chad, serves in the US Air Force with his wife, Julie, and are expecting their first son in March. Jake and Sandra's youngest son, Erik, is a business owner and entrepreneur and is engaged to his fiancée, Alli.

ROB "MUMBLES" POLUMBO

MAJOR GENERAL (RET)

Major General (Ret) Rob "Mumbles" Polumbo is a senior consultant for Two Blue Aces, a leadership consultancy that specializes in strategic reviews, business plan development, and leadership and mentor training. He also serves as a senior executive on the South Florida Defense Alliance and owner of

US Patriot Industries, an innovation and technology marketing company.

General Polumbo transitioned from the Air Force after thirty-three years of service. His career culminated as the special assistant to the commander, Air Force Reserve Command, Robins Air Force Base. General Polumbo assisted and advised the commander on the daily operations of the command, consisting of approximately seventy thousand citizen airmen and more than three hundred aircraft among three numbered air forces, providing air, space, and cyber support to combatant commands worldwide.

General Polumbo was a distinguished graduate of the U.S. Air Force Academy in 1984. During his fourteen years of active duty, he served as an instructor pilot, flight examiner, weapons officer, test and evaluation pilot, operations officer, and commander. Additionally, he served as the aide-de-camp to the Air Force chief of staff.

He transitioned to the Air Force Reserve Command in 1997, serving as a fighter squadron commander and later as a vice wing commander. During this time in 1999, he was hired by American Airlines and continues today to fly as a first officer on the Boeing 777 aircraft.

His senior executive positions included mobilization assistant and advisor to numerous commands and staffs, including the Air Force Warfare Center, Headquarters Air Combat Command, 7th Air Force, 12th Air Force, and Headquarters Air Force.

Rob earned a master's degree in aviation science from Embry-Riddle University in 1994 and is a command pilot with more than 4,300 hours of military aviation in all blocks of the F-16, including one hundred hours of combat time. He has also logged more than 8,300 flying hours in the Boeing 727, 757, 767, and 777 during his airline career.

JAMES "REV" JONES

MAJOR GENERAL (RET)

Major General (Ret) James "Rev" Jones is a senior consultant for Two Blue Aces, a leadership consultancy that specializes in strategic reviews, business plan development, and leadership and mentor training.

Rev transitioned from active military duty after more than thirty-one years of service. His military experience affords him the ability to provide senior-level strategy planning, leadership training, and solution-driven consulting to clients.

Prior to retiring from the Air Force, Rev served as the assistant deputy chief of staff for Operations, Plans and Requirements, where he was responsible to the secretary of the Air Force and the chief of staff for formulating policy supporting air, space, irregular warfare, counter-proliferation, homeland security, weather, and cyber operations. In his previous role as the Air Force's director of operations, General Jones helped determine operational requirements, capabilities, and training necessary to support national security objectives and military strategy.

Rev received his commission through Officer Training School in 1983 after graduating with a Bachelor of Science degree in music education from Louisiana Tech University in 1981. He gained high levels of credibility in the F-16 as an instructor pilot, chief of weapons and tactics, and an academic flight commander at the U.S. Air Force Weapons School.

He also has experience working with joint forces developing multi-service tactics, techniques, and procedures and determining munitions requirements for military operations. Following an operational command assignment of a fighter squadron, General Jones gained operational expertise in airborne command and control platforms, refueling aircraft, and intelligence, surveillance, and reconnaissance systems, giving General Jones a deep understanding of air power integration requirements.

Rev has commanded an operations group, the 380th Air Expeditionary Wing in Southwest Asia, the 116th Air Control Wing, and the 55th Wing, where he was recognized as Air Combat Command's best wing commander in 2009.

Prior to his final assignments at the Air Staff, he was the deputy commander of U.S. Air Forces Central Command, the deputy, Combined Force Air Component commander, U.S. Central Command, and the vice commander of the 9th Air Expeditionary Task Force.

General Jones is a command pilot with more than 2,700 flying hours in the RC-135, E-8C, KC-135R, E-3B/C, F-16A/B/C/D, T-38, and T-37.

General Jones also serves on the board of directors for a West Coast company that specializes in modeling and simulation systems and support services for 21st-century air, land, and sea synthetic training, and supports Air Force initiatives as an adjunct contract professor.

TOM "HONEZ" JONES

LIEUTENANT GENERAL (RET)

Lieutenant General (Ret) Noel T (Tom) "Honez" Jones is a senior consultant for Two Blue Aces, a leadership consultancy that specializes in strategic reviews, business plan development, and leadership and mentor training.

Tom transitioned from the Air Force after more than thirty-five years of service. His military experience and unique leadership positions make him extraordinarily qualified to provide focused solutions to client needs.

Tom retired as the vice commander of US Air Forces in Europe/Air Forces Africa. In that capacity, he was second in command for the air component to U.S. European Command and U.S. Africa Command. He was responsible for providing full-spectrum warfighting capabilities throughout the entire area of responsibility, which encompassed 104 countries in Europe, Africa, and the Arctic and Atlantic Oceans. He executed the organization, training, and equipping of over thirty-five thousand members at seven operating bases in five European nations.

General Jones entered active duty in 1980 as a graduate of the US Air Force Academy. He commanded at the squadron, group, and twice at the wing level—one in combat during Iraqi Freedom and one in peacetime as a brigadier general.

Tom had distinctly unique assignments as a general officer. As the commander at Luke Air Force Base, he led the Air Force's largest fighter wing, overseeing F-16 training for the Air Force with over two hundred aircraft and twenty-plus squadrons. He served for two years as the deputy director of the Central Security Service (military workforce for the National Security Agency), where he marshaled the efforts of sixteen thousand military cryptologists and cyber professionals in support of national and service intelligence requirements and participated in the standup of US Cyber Command.

He also served one year with the US Forces-Iraq in Baghdad as the director of plans and assessments (J-5). In this role, he directed planning to execute the presidential order to draw down all US forces from Iraq by the end of 2011 and led the assessment of all operations, combat and non-combat, to determine effectiveness in achieving the commander's stated objectives. This was the largest and most complex redeployment of US forces since WWII.

Tom later served as the director of Air Force requirements at the Pentagon where he established policy for operational capabilities-based requirements and supported commands in developing and evaluating the requirements for modernization programs including fighters, bombers, mobility aircraft, space systems, command and control, munitions, and cyber requirements.

Tom finished his career as a command pilot with over 3,600 total flying hours in the T-37, T-38, T-33, and all blocks of the F-16A/B/C/D. He had combat sorties in Operations Desert Fox, Southern Watch, and Iraqi Freedom.

RICHARD "BEEF" HADDAD

MAJOR GENERAL (RET)

Major General (Ret) Richard "Beef" Haddad is a senior consultant for Two Blue Aces, a leadership consultancy that specializes in strategic reviews, business plan development, and leadership and mentor training.

He retired as vice commander, Air Force Reserve Command. While working in the Air Force Reserve, he served as deputy chief in the Pentagon and directed Planning and Programming. Additionally, General Haddad sat on the Air Force board that plans, programs, budgets, and executes future war-fighting capabilities for the Air Force.

As vice commander in the Air Force Reserve Command, General Haddad directed the daily operations of the command, with 70,000 Citizen Airmen and more than three hundred aircraft among three numbered air forces, thirty-three flying wings, ten flying groups, and one space wing.

General Haddad is a veteran special operations pilot with hundreds of hours of combat flying in the AC130 Spectre Gunship and the MC130 Combat Talon during Operations Desert Storm, Enduring Freedom, and Iraqi Freedom. His aerial combat awards include three Distinguished Flying Crosses with "V for Valor" device and five Air Medals. He has deployed to combat zones eight times during his career.

Following September 11, General Haddad commanded the 711th Special Operations Squadron through Operations Enduring Freedom and Iraqi Freedom, during which the unit compiled more than five thousand combat hours of accident-free flying and is still recognized as the most combat-decorated Reserve flying unit.

General Haddad was commissioned through the Air Force Academy in 1981. He served in a variety of flying and command positions in the Air Force and Air Force Reserve. General Haddad was the first Air Force general officer nominated by the joint chiefs of staff to serve as commander, Special Operations Command Korea.

In his civilian job, he is an American Airlines pilot. He is married to Ginger, a retired Air Force colonel and judge advocate. They have two daughters, Alexandra, an attorney, and Victoria, MD, who is currently in her emergency medicine residency in Saginaw, Michigan, at Central Michigan University.

NOTES

9. STAND FIRMLY

1. Staff Sgt. Christopher Gross, "20 years later: Remembering the attack on Khobar Towers," U.S. Air Force, June 24, 2016, https://www.af.mil/News/Article-Display/Article/811370/20-years-later-remembering-the-attack-on-khobar-towers.
2. Norman Kempster, "Lying, Not Adultery, Is Female Pilot's Top Crime, AF Says," *Los Angeles Times*, May 22, 1997, http://articles.latimes.com/1997-05-22/news/mn-61313_1_air-force.

10. COURAGE IN THE LINE OF FIRE

1. Matthew B. Ridgway, "Leadership," *Military Review*, 1966.

13. THE CREDIBILITY OF PROFICIENCY

1. Wikipedia, s.v. "Billy Mitchell," last modified December 2, 2018, Wikipedia.org/wiki/Billy_Mitchell.
2. Dominick Pisano, "General William 'Billy' Mitchell and the Sinking of the Ostfriesland: A Consideration," last modified July 21, 2011, https://airandspace.si.edu/stories/editorial/general-william-%E2%80%9C-billy%E2%80%9D-mitchell-and-sinking-ostfriesland-consideration.
3. Pisano.
4. Mark St. John Erickson, "Battleship bombings of July 1921 marked milestone step in development of air power," *Daily Press*, July 20, 2018, www.dailypress.com/features/history/dp-langley-mitchell-bombings-201600420-story.html.
5. Rebecca Maksell, "The Billy Mitchell Court-Martial," *Air & Space Magazine*, July 2009.
6. "Gen. Billy Mitchell's Special Congressional Medal of Honor," National Museum of the US Air Force, April 9, 2015, www.nationalmuseum.af.mil/Visit/Museum-Exhibits/Fact-Sheets/Display/Article/198456/gen-billy-mitchells-special-congressional-medal-of-honor.
7. "Jimmy Doolittle," www.u-s-history.com/pages/h1691.html.
8. "Doolittle."

9. Wikipedia, s.v. "Jimmy Doolittle," last modified January 14, 2019, Wikipedia.org/wiki/Jimmy_Doolittle.

10. Wikipedia.

15. COWBOY COMPETENCE

1. *Multi-Command Manual 3-1, Mission Employment Volume 1 F-16 Tactics*

20. CARRY THE TORCH

1. John Gillespie Magee, Jr, "High Flight."

23. FIRED

1. Catherine Pulsifer, *Wings of Wisdom: Your Daily Guide to Benefit from Change, Profit from Failure, and Design Your Own Destiny!* (Amazon Digital Services LLC, 2013).

Made in the USA
Lexington, KY
29 September 2019